THE
Tammy Wynette
SOUTHERN
COOKBOOK

Photograph by Randee St. Nicholas

THE

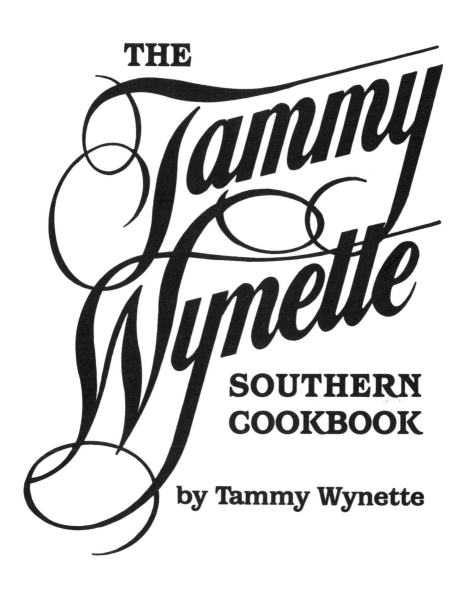

Tammy Wynette

SOUTHERN COOKBOOK

by Tammy Wynette

Pelican Publishing Company
Gretna 1990

Library of Congress Cataloging-in-Publication Data
Wynette, Tammy.
    The Tammy Wynette southern cookbook.
        p.   cm.
    ISBN 0-88289-734-9
    1. Cookery, American – Southern style.   I. Title.
TX715.2.S68W96   1989
641.5975 – dc20   89-16112
                                                                        CIP

*I would like to thank David Collins, George Richey, and
my many fans around the world for their photo contri-
butions.*

Manufactured in the United States of America
Published by Pelican Publishing Company, Inc.
1101 Monroe Street, Gretna, Louisiana 70053

Contents

Introduction

Dear Reader and Fellow Cook,

Thank you for buying my first-ever cookbook.

In these pages you will find many delicious, down-home country recipes unique to our Southern way of life. I hope that you will enjoy preparing and eating these dishes as much as I've enjoyed preparing them and presenting them in this book.

As many of you know already, I was born on a sharecropper farm in Itawamba County, Mississippi. We had no running water, no indoor plumbing, and no stove. We cooked over an open fireplace with water drawn and handcarried from a nearby spring. It was hard work and we worked hard – from the crack of dawn till the sun went down.

But, though we didn't have much of anything, one thing we *did* have a lot of was love. We were one big extended family, with my mother, my stepfather, my aunts, uncles, cousins, grandparents, and even a great-grandparent. We didn't have anything but we had each other. Despite our hard times and struggles we had a lot of happy moments and laughs. I have wonderful memories of those days and I wouldn't have traded them for the world.

In the years that have passed since then, I've performed on every continent, in hundreds of cities, and in nearly every state in the U.S. I've won many prestigious awards and have enjoyed great international acclaim. I've entertained in the White House numerous times, and before other heads of state, in addition to performing in some of the most famous concert halls in the world. Yet, despite all these honors, my roots are pure rural Mississippi. That was my home, my background, my upbringing, and my life. It still is.

For it was down on that farm that I learned the values and virtues I would carry throughout my life and my performing career: love of God, country, family, and the simple pleasures that make life so joyously worth living. Today I have a wonderful husband, five beautiful daughters, one wonderful son, and four grandchildren. To them I try to impart the same love I knew as a child, growing up on the farm. Although times have changed drastically and my children are scattered around, no longer living with us, we are still a close family. That, of all the things I've ever done in my life, is what I consider to be my greatest accomplishment.

But, just as music has always been a part of my life and an expression of my love for life, so has food. Growing up under the conditions we lived in, food was an important part of the love we shared for one another. I learned to cook at an early age from people like my mother, my grandmother, my great-grandmother, my aunts, and my cousins. In those days, with as little money as we had, we didn't enjoy the luxury and convenience of driving over to the supermarket and loading up the station wagon with everything we needed. Nearly everything we had to eat was prepared *from scratch* – using fresh, natural ingredients we either picked or slaughtered the same day. That was the basis of our existence.

To this day, I can still smell the wonderful aromas that drifted from the open windows and chimney of our little cabin as we picked cotton in the fields outside. I can close my eyes and remember sitting on the kitchen table watching my grandma and great-grandma laboring with love over a boiling kettle in the open fireplace. In the evenings, after it got too dark to work in the fields, our family would gather around the table, bow our heads, and thank God for what we had. Then we would eat. And chat. And trade stories of things that happened that day. And laugh. For as long as I live, I will treasure those precious moments shared around the dinner table eating simple but delicious food prepared with the most precious ingredient of all – love.

Many of the recipes in this book are from that time. I am especially grateful to my mother, Mildred Lee, for teaching them to me, and you will notice her name many times in these pages. Other recipes were taught to me by my grandmother, my great-grandmother, and several of my aunts and cousins. And, of course, I am indebted to many other people I have known since then for their recipes, and I have credited them accordingly as well.

Every time you try a new recipe it is like a new discovery, with all the adventure and excitement that goes along with that discovery. It may not always come out the way it should the first time, but you keep trying until you succeed in getting it right. The smiles and compliments are rewards that make it all worthwhile. I've burned my share of roasts and over-cooked my share of vegetables (who hasn't?) but I've learned from those experiences. Cooking is something I've always loved to do and, when you love something, you always want to give it your best effort. When I was a little girl, cooking was what I did to escape the rigors of picking cotton. Today I do it to relax and express my love for others.

My husband, George Richey (a wonderful cook himself, by the way), and I have entertained hundreds of people in our Nashville home. When these people, who have come to us in friendship drop by, I wouldn't dream of sending out for pizza or popping something pre-cooked into the microwave. I cook for them and then we sit down to enjoy it. That's the way it was in Itawamba County way back when; that's the way it is today. I wouldn't have it any other way.

As you read through these recipes and prepare the dishes contained here, don't be afraid to experiment. Ingredients, in most cases, are flexible and you can add more or less of something to suit your own tastes. I have listed the recipes in nine food categories and with them you can prepare a complete meal – from appetizers, to side dishes, to main courses, to desserts. Take my word for it, they're all delicious!

In closing, I have only one final word as you take *The Tammy Wynette Southern Cookbook* into the kitchen with you and open its pages next to your stove. Thank you!!

Love,

Tammy Wynette

THE
Tammy Wynette
SOUTHERN
COOKBOOK

Appetizers

MEXICAN EGGS A-LA-RICHEY

6 eggs
3 garden onions, diced
3 tablespoons Worcestershire sauce
2 slices American cheese
1/4 cup salsa sauce
1/2 cup milk

Mix ingredients together and scramble in large skillet with 1/2 stick of butter.

This was taught to me by my husband, George Richey, and is a special treat in our home. Everything goes in this except the kitchen sink. It's a wonderful way to fix eggs.

BREAKFAST MAIN DISH

1 lb. sausage, cooked & crumbled
1 cup grated cheddar cheese
1 cup sweet milk
1/2 teaspoon salt
3 slices of bread, cubed
4 eggs, beaten
1/2 teaspoon milk

Mix altogether. Put in greased 9x13 pan. Refrigerate overnight. Bake at 350 degrees for 35 minutes. Cut into squares and serve hot. (May be frozen until ready to cook but thaw in refrigerator overnight before baking.)

Taught to me by Sandra and Gerald Jetton.

FARMERS VEGETABLE SOUP

5 fresh tomatoes, diced or quartered
(or 2 small cans of stewed
tomatoes)
1/2 cup lima beans
1/2 cup Niblets corn
4 sliced, fresh okra pods
(or 1/2 frozen)
5 potatoes, quartered
1 cup chopped cabbage
2 tablespoons sugar
Salt and pepper

Add enough water to completely cover the combined mixture. Add sugar. Salt and pepper to taste. Cook on medium heat until all vegetables are tender. You can always add more water to make it thinner.

This is a dish I put together while living on our farm in Mississippi. I used all fresh vegetables and it's a favorite of mine today. On the farm we raised almost everything we cooked. Sure is different today.

When I married at seventeen, I lived in a log house owned by my grandfather. I had no electricity, no running water, no plumbing, and no stove. I cooked in a big iron black pot inside my fireplace and I cooked a lot of soup.

FRESH GARDEN SALAD

2 large tomatoes, chopped fine
2 large onions, chopped fine
1/4 cup vinegar
2 tablespoons sugar
1 12oz. jar hot salsa sauce
2 4oz. cans chopped green chiles
3 medium cucumbers, chopped fine
2 cloves garlic, chopped fine
1/2 cup oil (Mazola)
1 can 28 oz. tomatoes, drained,
  chopped fine

Mix all ingredients, serve with tortilla chips or serve as a dinner relish. This salsa will refrigerate for a week or two.

Taught to me by my friend Cleta Hillygus.

DUMP SALAD

1 large box orange Jell-o
1 medium container cottage cheese
9 oz. Cool Whip
1 can pineapple chunks
1 can mandarin oranges

Stir dry Jell-o into cottage cheese. Mix well. Add pineapple and oranges. Gently fold in Cool Whip. Refrigerate overnight.

Taught to me by my niece Lisa Meier Hadden.

24 HOUR SALAD

1 head lettuce
1 package cleaned, fresh spinach
3 or 4 fresh garden onions
1 head cauliflower (chopped)
Shredded cheese
1 cup Miracle Whip
1/4 cup sugar
1/2 cup bacon bits
1/3 cup parmesan cheese

Place 1 layer of lettuce in a large salad bowl. Add a layer of fresh spinach. Dice garden onions and place on top of the spinach. Add 1 layer of chopped cauliflower and sprinkle parmesan cheese to form another layer. Sprinkle bacon bits on top of that layer.

When all layers are finished spread sugar on top, then spread Miracle Whip. Cover with shredded cheese.

Cover with Saran Wrap and chill in refrigerator for 24 hours. Toss and serve.

My very favorite salad!

CRANBERRY SALAD

1 lb. fresh cranberries, ground
1 1/2 cups sugar
1 can crushed pineapple
  (medium-sized, drained)
1/2 lb. miniature marshmallows
1 cup walnuts, diced
1 pint whipping cream, whipped

Mix ground cranberries, pineapples, and sugar and refrigerate overnight. Add rest of ingredients an hour before serving.

Taught to me by my sister-in-law Marie Meier.

NEXT DAY SALAD

1 firm head lettuce (tear to bite size)
4 hard-boiled eggs, diced
1/2 cup bell pepper, diced
1/2 cup celery, chopped
1 can drained green peas
1 onion, chopped
8 slices bacon, fried and chopped
4 oz. grated cheddar cheese

Layer first 7 ingredients starting with lettuce.

2 cups Miracle Whip: spread over top of salad to seal ingredients
2 tablespoons sugar: sprinkle over Miracle Whip

Top with grated cheese. Refrigerate until next day.

Taught to me by my sister-in-law Marie Meier.

WALDORF SALAD

1/2 cup raisins
1/2 cup miniature marshmallows
1 cup chopped celery
1 teaspoon lemon juice
2 tablespoons sugar
1/4 cup mayonnaise
1/2 cup whipped cream
1/2 cup broken nuts
Dash of salt
2 cups tart apples, diced

Sprinkle apples with salt and sugar. Add lemon juice, nuts, and celery. Fold whipped cream and mayonnaise gently into apple mixture. Add raisins and marshmallows.

Taught to me by my mother Mildred Lee.

POTATO SALAD

6 quartered potatoes, cooked
3 tablespoons mustard
2 teaspoons salt
2 teaspoons pepper
1 cup diced celery
4 hard-boiled eggs, chopped
1 cup onions, diced
1 1/2 cups Miracle Whip

Cook potatoes until tender. Drain and let cool. Mix all ingredients together in large bowl. Serve on bed of lettuce or plain.

3 BEAN SALAD

1 can cut green beans
1 can wax beans
1 can kidney beans, washed
1 red onion, sliced
1 white onion, sliced
1 bell pepper, sliced

Dissolve the following and pour over above mixture:

3/4 cup sugar
2/3 cup tarragon vinegar
1/3 cup salad oil
1 teaspoon salt
1/4 teaspoon pepper

Refrigerate 24 hours, stirring occasionally.

Taught to me by my mother Mildred Lee.

HOMEMADE CHICKEN SALAD

1 cut up fryer
1/2 cup diced celery
1 diced onion
Salt and pepper to taste
3 hard-boiled eggs, diced
3/4 cup Miracle Whip

Boil fryer in stewer, covered with water, salt, and black pepper until chicken is well done. Remove from heat, drain and let cool. When cool enough to handle, pull all chicken off the bones (being careful not to get any small bones into mixture) and place in bowl. Add celery, onions, eggs, and Miracle Whip. Mix well. Cool and serve.

FRUIT SALAD
AND FRUIT DRESSING

1 can mandarin oranges
1 can pineapple chunks
1 jar maraschino cherries
2 apples, peeled and diced
2 pears, peeled and diced
2 bananas, sliced
2 teaspoons fruit pectin
1 cup confectioners sugar

DRESSING

1 tablespoon flour
1/2 tablespoon mace
1/2 tablespoon paprika
1/2 cup honey
1 egg
1/2 cup pineapple juice
3 tablespoons lime juice
1 1/2 tablespoons poppy seeds

Add fruit pectin and confectioners sugar to the fruit. Put flour, mace, paprika, and 1 tablespoon of the honey into a saucepan. Stir until well combined. Add remaining honey, egg, juices, and poppy seeds. Cook over low heat, stirring until slightly thick. Chill and serve with fresh or canned fruit.

Note: Adding fruit pectin keeps the fruit from discoloring.

KRAUT SALAD

1 large can kraut
1 cup chopped celery
1 large onion, chopped
1 large green pepper, diced
Dash of garlic salt
Pimento for color

Mix all ingredients and make dressing.

DRESSING

1/2 cup salad oil
1/2 cup vinegar
1 cup sugar
1 teaspoon salt
1/2 teaspoon celery seed

Mix well and pour over vegetables. Chill all day or overnight before serving.

SALAD WITH
TUNA AND SALMON

1 layer lettuce
1 layer spinach
1 layer chopped green onions
1/2 cup bacon bits
1 can drained tuna
1 can salmon

Toss all ingredients in large bowl and serve with favorite salad dressing.

TUNA SALAD (1)

In a medium or large mixing bowl rub half of a garlic clove thoroughly around sides of bowl. As you prepare the following ingredients add them to bowl.

2-6 1/2 oz. cans spring water tuna
2 spears or 1/2 of pickle
  (dill or sweet)
1 dozen large black pitted olives,
  chopped
3 soup spoons of wheat germ
2 medium garlic cloves,
  chopped extra fine
3 rounded medium serving spoons
  mayonnaise or salad dressing
  (add more later if needed)
1 small or medium-sized onion,
  chopped fine
1 medium-sized heart of celery
  & leaves, chopped fine
4 hard-boiled eggs,
  chopped medium fine
1 level teaspoon mustard
1 soup spoon Worcestershire sauce

Serve on a bed of lettuce or with unsalted top crackers. Also very good served with rye bread and cheese of your choice. Serves 6 to 8.

Taught to me by my brother-in-law Bill Whitlach.

TUNA SALAD (2)

**2 cans Bumble Bee Chunk
White Tuna
6 to 8 sweet midget pickles, diced
1/2 medium-sized onion, diced
3 boiled eggs, diced
1/2 apple, diced
1/2 cup mayonnaise or Miracle Whip**

Combine all ingredients and serve as salad or sandwich.

An old Itawamba County recipe.

COLE SLAW

**1 medium cabbage
1 medium bell pepper
1 medium onion
1 medium carrot**

Grate these vegetables in large bowl. Add 2 teaspoons salt to 1 cup boiling water. Pour over grated vegetables and let stand 1 hour. Drain thoroughly.

**1/2 cup vinegar
1/2 cup oil
1 teaspoon mustard seed
1/2 cup sugar
1 teaspoon celery seed**

Mix thoroughly. Pour over the grated vegetables, mix well, and refrigerate. This slaw will keep two or three days.

Taught to me by my sister-in-law Vi Whitlatch.

REFRIGERATOR SLAW

1 medium head cabbage, grated
1/2 green pepper, chopped
  (more or less as desired)
1/4 onion, chopped

SYRUP

1 cup sugar
1 cup vinegar
1 teaspoon salt
1 teaspoon mustard seed
1/2 teaspoon turmeric

Bring syrup to a boil. Toss vegetables together. Pour hot syrup over vegetables. Pack in jars if convenient. Cool and store in refrigerator overnight. Will keep 2 or 3 weeks in refrigerator.

IDEAS FOR PARTY SANDWICHES

Cooked ground ham, ground celery, sweet pickles, and mayonnaise.

Cooked liver ground with fried bacon, sautéed onions, celery, and mayonnaise.

Cooked chicken ground with hard cooked eggs, sweet pickles, celery, and mayonnaise.

To one 3 oz. package of cream cheese, add any of the following combinations:

Chopped or ground pecans and ripe olives.

Chopped or ground cucumbers, onion juice, ground celery, and mayonnaise.

Chopped or ground pecans, drained crushed pineapple, and a little mayonnaise.

Chopped or ground pecans, minced onion, and 1 teaspoon Roquefort cheese.

Breads

SIMPLE BUTTERMILK BISCUITS

2 cups self-rising flour, sifted
1/4 teaspoon baking soda
1/4 cup shortening
7/8 cup buttermilk

Cut or rub shortening into flour and soda until particles are as fine as coarse crumbs. Add buttermilk and stir in with fork. Turn dough onto lightly floured board and knead till smooth. Roll dough out about 1/2-inch thick and cut with floured cutter or juice glass. Place on lightly greased baking sheet and refrigerate till morning. Before serving, pop into preheated 450 degree oven for 10 to 12 minutes.

Taught to me by my mother, Mildred Lee. About six years ago I had surgery when we lived in Florida. I had a 24-hour private duty nurse. I just couldn't seem to get an appetite for anything, but Richey knew I loved homemade biscuits from scratch. He asked how to make them and one morning I got up and walked into the kitchen. There was flour everywhere. Richey had it from head to toe all over him. From that day on he knew how to make biscuits. He now makes them much better than me, but he had a good teacher.

YEAST BISCUITS

5 cups self-rising flour
1 scant cup oil
1 package quick rise yeast
2 cups buttermilk
1 teaspoon soda
2 teaspoons sugar

Dissolve yeast in 1/4 cup warm water. Mix with all other ingredients. Put in a large bowl since the mixture rises. Refrigerate (it will keep about 2 weeks). Remove the desired amount; shape and place on an ungreased baking sheet. Bake at 400 degrees for 12-15 minutes.

BEER BISCUITS

3 cups Bisquick
2 tablespoons sugar
1 12 oz. can of beer

Mix together with fork and pour into greased muffin pan. Bake at 400 degrees for 15 or 20 minutes. Brush with butter when removing from oven. Makes 12 large rolls.

BLACK SKILLET CORN BREAD

2 cups plain cornmeal
***1 teaspoon soda**
***1 teaspoon salt**
2 tablespoons flour
2 eggs
2 cups buttermilk
2 tablespoons (more or less)
   corn oil

Preheat oven to 450 degrees. Grease skillet and heat. Combine cornmeal, soda, salt, and flour. Add lightly beaten eggs, buttermilk, and corn oil. Bake in hot oven (450 degrees) about 30 minutes.

*If using self-rising meal omit soda and salt

Taught to me by my mother, Mildred Lee. One day when I was about 9 years old, she gave me the choice of staying home and cooking or working in the fields picking cotton. My choice was to cook. I prepared a meal consisting of meatloaf, pinto beans, fried okra, and cornbread. I made the mistake of putting green cake coloring in the cornbread to make it a pretty color. It didn't change the taste but Peepaw wouldn't eat it. He said he knew it was okay but it looked like poison!

SOUR CREAM CORNBREAD

1 1/2 cups self-rising cornmeal
3/4 cup Wesson Oil
2 eggs
1 small can cream corn
1/2 cup sour cream
1 small onion, minced

Mix and pour into greased iron skillet. Bake at 325 degrees for 30 minutes.

Taught to me by Barbara Russell.

MEXICAN CORNBREAD (1)

1 1/2 cups meal
1/2 cup flour
3 eggs
1 jalapeño pepper, chopped fine
   or grated (remove seeds)
1 large grated onion
1/2 cup Wesson Oil
   (or bacon drippings)
2 1/2 cups grated cheddar cheese
1 can Mexicorn (small can)

Mix all ingredients and bake at 375 degrees for about 35 minutes.

Taught to me by my mother Mildred Lee.

MEXICAN CORNBREAD (2)

1 can chopped green chilés
1 cup cornmeal
1 cup milk
1/2 cup salad oil
2 eggs
1 small can cream-style corn
1/2 tsp. baking powder
1/2 tsp. salt
1 chopped onion (small to medium)
1 cup longhorn cheese (grated)

Mix all ingredients together and pour into greased 9-inch square pan. Bake for 1 hour at 350 degrees. Yield: 10 servings.

Note: You can also add a few jalapeños if you like it hot.

This was given to me by Steve Gatlin, one of the Gatlin Brothers, and it's the best I've ever tried. Thanks Steve!

CORNBREAD FRITTERS

2 cups self-rising cornmeal
2 eggs
1 1/2 cups hot water

Mix together and fry in a skillet with 1/2 cup cooking oil. Have oil hot and fry like pancakes, 3 or 4 minutes on each side or until golden-brown. Serve with fresh vegetables.

HUSH PUPPIES

2 eggs
1 cup sweet milk
1 1/4 cups cornmeal
3/4 cup flour
5 teaspoons soda
Salt to taste
1/2 cup diced onion
1 teaspoon mustard
1 teaspoon black pepper

Mix all ingredients together, drop by tablespoons into deep, hot fat. Brown, drain, and serve with fish.

This is a wonderful Southern recipe. My mother makes the best. The difference (I think) is the soda that she uses.

BUTTER ROLLS

Use standard dough recipe (see index) and roll into an area approximately 8 inches wide and 8 inches long. Roll thin and generously apply squeeze butter, covering the entire dough area. Smooth and sprinkle 1 1/2 cups of sugar. Roll thin and in a cylinder roll. Let cool or serve hot with ice cream or Cool Whip as toppings or serve plain.

An old Itawamba County recipe.

PRUNE ROLLS
AND WHITE SAUCE

1 package of dried prunes
1 1/2 cups of sugar

Place 1 package of dried prunes in a deep sauce pan. Cover with water and cook until tender and until water has cooked down. Be careful that the cooked prunes are dry (not watery). Remove from heat and set aside.

Using the recipe for pastry or dough, roll out a piece of dough approximately 10″ wide and 10″ long. When prunes are cooled, pour on dough leaving 1″ around the edges. Roll into cylinder shape and place in ovenproof greased dish. Bake until golden brown on 350 degrees. Remove from oven and cool.

WHITE SAUCE

1/2 cup flour
1 1/2 cups milk
1 cup sugar
1 teaspoon vanilla flavoring

Mix and heat white sauce and pour over cooked prune roll.

This may not sound like a very good dish but, believe me, everyone I've cooked it for has gone nuts over it. It's delicious!

HOMEMADE ROLLS
(quick)

1 cake yeast
2 cups lukewarm water
1 egg
1 teaspoon salt
1/2 cup sugar
3/4 cup lard
6 cups plain flour

Beat egg, sugar, and salt like batter for cake. Dissolve yeast in 1 cup lukewarm water, and add to egg mixture. Soften lard in 1 cup of lukewarm water, then mix all ingredients together, adding 6 cups of flour.

Roll out and place in buttered pan and let rise for 2 1/2 hours. Can be frozen or kept in refrigerator covered well for several days.

I put these in the refrigerator in muffin pans just ready to rise. I take them out 2 hours before using.

Yields 3 dozen.

Taught to me by my mother Mildred Lee.

HOMEMADE ROLLS

5 1/2 cups plain flour
1/2 teaspoon salt
3/4 cup sugar
1 egg, beaten
3/4 cup shortening
1 package yeast
1 to 1 1/2 cups warm water

Dissolve yeast in 1/4 cup warm water and set aside.

Blend sugar, flour, and salt. Add shortening and work with a fork until crumbly. Add egg. Pour yeast mixture over all and stir well. Add 1 to 1 1/2 cups warm water and stir until creamy. Pinch off into rolls and let rise in a warm place 3 or 4 hours. May be stored in refrigerator for up to one week. Bake at 400 degrees for about 20 minutes or until brown.

24-HOUR HAMBURGER ROLLS

Boil 4 cups water and 1 3/4 cups sugar for five minutes. Add 1 cup lard and 1 tablespoon salt, and let cool for one hour.

Add 1 package yeast dissolved in 1/4 cup warm water and 1 tablespoon sugar. Add this and 3 beaten eggs to 12 1/2 cups flour, and add to first mixture.

All this should be done by 11 a.m. Stir down at 4 p.m. and 6 p.m. Make into rolls and put on greased pans at 9 p.m. Let rise overnight. Bake at 350 degrees for 18-20 minutes.

FAST YEAST ROLLS

1 package yeast
1 cup warm water
4 1/2 tablespoons sugar
1 1/2 tablespoons shortening

Mix ingredients and add enough flour (self-rising) to make dough pliable. Form rolls to size desired and brush with melted butter. Let stand in warm place for 40 minutes. Bake at 375 degrees until brown.

BANANA NUT LOAF

2/3 cup sugar
2 eggs
1 cup mashed ripe bananas
1/4 teaspoon soda
1/3 cup soft shortening
3 tablespoons buttermilk
2 cups sifted self-rising flour
1/2 cup chopped nuts

Grease an 8 1/2 x 2 1/2-inch loaf pan. Mix together thoroughly: sugar, shortening, and eggs. Stir in buttermilk, mashed bananas, flour, then stir in soda, and add chopped nuts. Turn batter into prepared pan. Bake 50 to 60 minutes. Yield: 1 loaf.

"A classic – especially good with fruit salad; a lunch box favorite."

BUTTERMILK
REFRIGERATOR ROLLS

1 cake yeast
5 cups flour
2 cups buttermilk
3 tablespoons shortening
1 teaspoon salt
1/4 teaspoon baking powder
1/4 teaspoon soda
3 tablespoons sugar

Dissolve yeast in buttermilk. Combine dry ingredients in large bowl. Cut in shortening. Add buttermilk with yeast. Store in refrigerator overnight or at least several hours. Remove from refrigerator several hours before baking. Shape rolls as desired. Bake at 400 degrees for 20 minutes.

DROP ROLLS

1 package dry yeast
2 cups warm water
1/4 cup sugar
1/2 cup shortening
1 egg
4 cups self-rising flour

Mix well. Place dough in refrigerator until ready to bake. Will last for approximately one week.

Drop into greased muffin pan. Bake at 400 degrees until brown.

POPPY SEED BREAD

Grease and flour 2 loaf pans. Preheat oven to 325 degrees.

2 cups sugar
1 1/3 cups oil
1 1/2 cups milk
3 eggs

Mix sugar and oil. Add eggs one at a time, add milk.

ADD:

3 cups sifted self-rising flour
1 1/2 tablespoons poppy seeds
1 1/2 teaspoons vanilla
2 teaspoons almond flavoring

Beat 2 minutes. Bake one hour at 325 degrees.

Taught to me by Sandra and Gerald Jetton.

INDIA'S FRIED BREAD
(from London)

2 cups flour
1 teaspoon salt
1/4 cup melted butter
6 tablespoons water
1 1/2 cups hot oil

Mix flour, salt, and butter into bowl. Stir in water. Blend thoroughly with hands. Knead until firm on flat floured surface. Roll dough very thin. Cut in 4 inch circles. Fry in hot, deep oil.

FRENCH ONION BREAD

5 1/2 to 6 cups all-purpose flour
2 packages active dry yeast
1 envelope dry onion soup mix
   (4-6 serving)
2 tablespoons sugar
2 tablespoons shortening
Corn meal
1 beaten egg white
1 teaspoon salt

In large mixer bowl combine 2 1/2 cups of the flour and the yeast. In saucepan combine 2 1/4 cups water and soup mix. Simmer, covered, for 10 minutes. Stir in sugar, shortening, and salt. Add to dry mixture. Beat at low speed with mixer for 1/2 minute, scraping bowl. Beat 3 minutes at high speed. Stir in enough remaining flour to make a moderately stiff dough.

Knead on floured surface until smooth (8-10 minutes). Shape into ball. Place in greased bowl; turn once. Cover; let rise in warm place till double (about 1 hour). Punch down; divide in half. Cover; let rest 10 minutes. Shape into 2 long loaves, tapering ends. Place on greased baking sheet sprinkled with corn meal. Gash tops diagonally, 1/4 inch deep. Cover; let rise till double (about 30 minutes). Bake at 375 degrees for 20 minutes. Brush with mixture of egg white and 1 tablespoon water. Bake 10-15 minutes longer. Remove from baking sheet; cool. Makes 2 loaves.

Goes great with lasagna, spaghetti, and other Italian dishes.

PUMPKIN BREAD

3 1/2 cups flour (self-rising)
1 teaspoon cinnamon
3 1/2 cups sugar
1 cup vegetable oil
1 cup chopped nuts
1 teaspoon nutmeg
4 eggs, beaten
2 1/2 cups mashed pumpkin
1 teaspoon vanilla

Mix dry ingredients, blend other ingredients except nuts. Mix alternately and add nuts. Grease 2 bundt pans and fill. Bake approximately 45 minutes at 350 degrees.

ZUCCHINI BREAD

2 1/2 cups grated zucchini
3 eggs
1 cup oil
2 cups sugar
3 cups plain flour
3 teaspoons vanilla
1 teaspoon soda
1 teaspoon salt
3 teaspoons cinnamon
1 teaspoon baking powder

Mix sugar, oil, eggs, and vanilla. Add baking powder, soda, salt, and cinnamon to flour and sugar mixture. Add zucchini and mix well. Pour into greased and floured loaf pan. Bake at 350 degrees for 55 minutes.

Taught to me by my mother Mildred Lee.

AVERAGE PIE DOUGH
Pastry or Dough

2 1/2 cups self-rising dough
1 cup Crisco
3/4 cup water

This mixture can be used for dumplings, pie crust, etc. Combine flour, Crisco, and water. Form a ball and knead until firm, occasionally sprinkling the dough with flour to keep it from being sticky. Roll thin and slice. Standard dough mixture.

For pie crust, divide in half and roll thin in pieces the size of an 8- or 9-inch pie pan.

CHICKEN (or HAM)
AND DUMPLIN'S

1 whole cut up frying chicken
or 1 2 lb. canned ham

Place cut up chicken into deep saucepan. Cover with water and cook on medium heat until tender. Salt and pepper to taste. Use standard dough or pastry recipe for dumplin's. Roll dough very thin and cut into 1-inch strips. Slowly drop dough strips into cooked chicken. Make dumplin's as thick as desired. This recipe can also be used with ham. Use diced canned ham instead of chicken.

My mother and her mother (Mildred Lee and Flora Russell) taught me how to prepare this dish. Since we raised our own pork and chickens we had this quite often.

Beverages

HOT RUSSIAN TEA

1 gallon water
3 small tea bags
1 16 oz. frozen orange juice
1 16 oz. frozen lemonade
2 sticks cinnamon
2 whole cloves
2 cups sugar

Boil tea bags, cloves, and cinnamon in water for 2 minutes. Remove tea bags, cloves, and cinnamon. Add sugar and juices, mix, and serve hot. Makes 1 gallon.

CARD PLAYING TEA

1/2 cup instant tea or brewed tea
1 1/2 cups sugar
1 cup Tang
1 package lemonade mix
3/4 teaspoons cinnamon

Mix well, store in jars. Use 3 teaspoons per cup and serve hot.

There is an old card game known as Rook. It is very popular in our home. As far back as probably 60 years ago or longer, it was played. This is served sometimes during one of our "mad games."

WEDDING PUNCH

1 large can of Hawaiian Punch
1 large can of pineapple juice
1 large can of apple juice
1 bottle of pink champagne

Mix together, pour into punch bowl over ice. Chill and serve.

This punch has been served at Gwen's, Jackie's, and Tina's weddings, and also at mine. It's good!

HOT CHOCOLATE MIX

1 8 qt. box powdered milk
1 1 lb. box Nestlé's Quik or
  Hershey's Instant Cocoa
1 6 oz. jar instant creamer
1/2 1 lb. box powdered sugar

Mix together. Makes about 1 gallon mix. Use 1/3 cup mix to each cup of hot milk.

Pasta

ZUCCHINI – EGGPLANT LASAGNE

3 medium zucchini, sliced crosswise
1 eggplant, peeled and sliced
crosswise
1 large green pepper, sliced in strips
1 large onion
1 envelope spaghetti sauce
15 oz. can tomato sauce
(make sauce like recipe
says on the can)
1 large carton cottage cheese
(don't need all)
Parmesan cheese
6 oz. Mozzarella cheese

Coat zucchini slices and eggplant with flour. Brown lightly in oil. Set aside. Stir-fry pepper and onions till slightly limp. Layer casserole dish (about 2 quart size) as follows: spaghetti sauce, zucchini, eggplant, cottage cheese, green pepper and onion, mozzarella cheese, parmesan. Repeat. End with spaghetti sauce and parmesan. Bake at 350 degrees for 45 minutes.

SPAGHETTI AND MEATBALLS

3/4 lb. ground beef
1/2 lb. ground pork
1/4 lb. veal
3 slices whole wheat bread
1/2 cup milk or meat stock
1 medium onion
1 clove garlic
1/2 green pepper
Fistful parsley
1/2 lemon rind
2 eggs
1 teaspoon salt
1 teaspoon pepper
Pinch of cloves and nutmeg
2 bay leaves

Soak bread in milk or stock while you finely chop up onion, garlic, pepper, and parsley and grate lemon. Squeeze liquid from bread and mix meat, bread, vegetables, eggs, and seasonings (except bay leaves) all together. Cover and let stand for 1 hour to develop flavors. Then shape into balls, grease bottom of shallow roasting pan with oil, put in meatballs and bay leaves, and bake in 450-degree oven for 15 minutes, brush with oil, and bake another 15 minutes.

SAUCE

1/4 cup salad oil
1/2 lb. ground beef
1 clove garlic
Parsley
1/4 cup white wine
Salt and pepper
1 can tomato puree
1 4 oz. can tomato paste
1/2 cup water
1/2 cup parmesan cheese

To make sauce, brown meat and garlic in oil, pour in wine, and simmer 10 minutes. Add salt, pepper, parsley and tomato mixtures, and water and cook 30 minutes. Add meatballs to sauce and cook gently 1 hour longer. Serve over cooked spaghetti and sprinkle with parmesan cheese. Serves 6.

PILAF

1/4-1/2 large package vermicelli
  (thin spaghetti)
3 tablespoons butter
1 cup rice (Uncle Ben's), cooked
2 1/2 cups chicken broth
Pieces of chicken, turkey, or
  mushrooms or combination

Brown vermicelli in 1 tablespoon butter. Add meat and/or mushrooms. Add cooked rice and stir. Add chicken broth and simmer on low heat. Just before the broth is completely absorbed, put in the remaining 2 tablespoons butter.

CHICKEN SPAGHETTI

1 whole chicken or
   boneless chicken breast
1 large onion
3 stalks celery
1 bell pepper
Spaghetti
1 can tomato paste
1 can tomato sauce
Mushrooms (optional)
Garlic salt, salt & pepper to taste
Jack cheese, grated
Cheddar cheese, grated
Italian seasoning to taste
Marjoram to taste

Boil chicken until tender. Save broth to cook spaghetti. Cut up cooked chicken into small pieces and add to cooked spaghetti in skillet. Add tomato sauce and paste. In separate skillet sauté onion, bell pepper, and celery. Add this to other ingredients. Add water (1/2 cup or so), add all seasonings and simmer for 20-30 minutes.

Pour into casserole dish. Sprinkle Jack cheese over top – then cheddar cheese. Preheat oven to 350 degrees. Cook for 30-40 minutes.

Taught to me by my sister-in-law Marie Meier.

CHEESE AND MACARONI

1 lb. processed American cheese, sliced
1 teaspoon salt
1/8 teaspoon white pepper
1 8 oz. (cooked and drained) package of elbow macaroni
6 tablespoons margarine
6 tablespoons flour
1/2 teaspoon onion salt
3 cups milk

Grease crock pot, prepare sauce, gradually stirring in cheese. Cook macaroni per package directions. Pour macaroni into crock pot. Pour sauce over the macaroni. Stir, cover, and cook on low for 1 hour.

Taught to me by my niece Brenda Kennedy.

Fish 'N' Fowl

MEXICAN CHICKEN

1 chicken boiled with meat taken off bones
1 package Doritos chips
1 cup diced onion
1 can celery soup
1 can cream of chicken soup
1 cup chicken stock
   (liquid from boiled chicken)
1 can stewed tomatoes
1 cup shredded cheese

Layer chicken, Doritos, and onions in ovenproof baking dish. Mix tomatoes and soups. Pour over layers. Sprinkle cheese over layers. Bake at 325 degrees for 1 hour, covered with foil.

BRENDA'S CHICKEN

6 boneless chicken breasts
1 can cream of mushroom soup
1 can milk
Parsley
1 can creamy onion soup
1 can sliced mushrooms
Garlic salt or fresh garlic

Season chicken breast with salt, pepper, and garlic salt. Mix all other ingredients together and pour over chicken. Sprinkle chicken with parsley. Bake at 350 degrees for 1 hour or until chicken is tender.

A California dish taught to me by my niece, Brenda Meier.

HOMEMADE CHICKEN POT PIE

Ingredients will make enough for Pyrex dish size (approximate) 12 x 8 x 2. Dissolve 1 package dry yeast in 1/4 cup warm water. Set aside, mix dry ingredients in order below:

2 1/2 cups all-purpose flour
1/2 teaspoon baking soda
1 teaspoon baking powder
1 teaspoon salt
1/8 cup sugar

Cut in 1/2 cup any good shortening, as you would for pie crust – then add 1 cup buttermilk and the water-yeast mixture. Mix thoroughly. Cover the bowl. Let rise while preparing filling.

Precook boiling chicken or fryer. When chilled pick all meat from bone, saving the broth.

Prepare vegetables: 4 large pieces of celery, diced, and 4 or 5 medium carrots, diced. Cook until tender and drain off water. Strain chicken broth and pour over carrots and celery. Add to this one can drained sweet green peas. Bring to a slow boil. Add 3 tablespoons cornstarch to small amount of water in mixing cup and add to vegetable mixture, stirring constantly until thick. Salt to taste. Remove from heat, add diced cold chicken.

Take 1/3 of the dough, roll out on floured board like pie dough. Cover bottom of baking dish. Flute around the edges to prevent shrinkage. Add the chicken and vegetable mixture. Roll out remainder of dough, cutting as you would for biscuits. (No need to let rise again, as the warm filling will cause the biscuits to rise.) Place biscuits on top of filling (makes 12 to 15 biscuits) and place in preheated 350-degree oven. Takes about 15-20 minutes for the biscuits to turn a golden brown. They will rise above the dish.

This is another dish I used to prepare before going on the road and leave for my children. It's a full meal in one dish.

CHICKEN DIVAN

8 chicken breasts (boiled)
1 can cream of chicken soup and
   1 cup broth
2 tablespoons lemon juice
1 package Pepperidge Farms Bread
   Crumbs (buttered)
3 packages frozen broccoli spears
   (cooked)
2/3 cup mayonnaise
1/2 cup grated cheese

Place broccoli spears in bottom of baking dish. Lay cubed chicken over broccoli. Pour remaining ingredients over this. Sprinkle bread crumbs on top and cook at 350 degrees for 20-30 minutes.

A dish from Arkansas taught to me by my niece, Brenda Kennedy.

GRILLED LEMON CHICKEN

**6 boneless chicken breasts
  marinated in:
  3/4 cup Worcestershire
  3/4 cup wine and pepper sauce
  salt and pepper to taste
1/2 cup melted butter
4 oz. lemon juice
Garlic powder
Parsley**

Sprinkle lightly with garlic powder and parsley. Put breasts on grill and brush both sides with butter throughout the 45-minute cooking time. Brush periodically with lemon juice and butter regularly throughout the cooking time. Brush on the remains of the marinating sauce. For decoration, sprinkle with parsley.

Another recipe from my husband, George Richey. Between Richey and my cook, Cleta Hillygus, I don't have to cook if I don't want to. Isn't that wonderful?

VIVA LA CHICKEN
TORTILLA CASSEROLE

**4 whole chicken breasts, cooked
  (turkey can be used)
1 can cream of mushroom soup
1 onion, chopped or grated
  (can use dry minced)
1/2 to 1 lb. grated tillamook cheese
1 dozen corn tortillas
1 can cream of chicken soup
1 cup milk
3 cans Ortega green chili salsa (7 oz.)**

Cut or tear tortillas into small pieces. Mix soups, milk, onion, and salsa. Oil shallow baking dish. Place layer of tortillas, layer of diced chicken and layer of soup mixture. Sprinkle a little cheese then start another layer. (Usually makes three layers.) End up with soup mixture and top with generous layer of cheese. Let stand in refrigerator 24 hours to blend flavors. Bake in 300-degree oven for 1 to 1 1/2 hours, until bubbly hot. This casserole freezes beautifully.

Taught to me by my sister-in-law Vi Whitlatch.

MISSISSIPPI FRIED CHICKEN

2 or 3 lb. chicken, cut into pieces
1 egg, beaten in 1/4 cup cold water
1 cup cold water
1 cup buttermilk
1 teaspoon paprika
Pinch of allspice
Pinch of ginger
1/4 teaspoon black pepper
2 teaspoons salt
Flour (to dredge chicken)
1/2 cup oil or Crisco
1 stick oleo

In medium-sized bowl, put beaten egg, water and milk and blend. When blended add paprika, allspice, ginger, black pepper, and salt. Put chicken pieces in mixture and turn to cover. Let stand at room temperature.

In large skillet, heat oil and oleo. Place floured pieces of chicken in hot grease. Brown on one side, turn, and brown on the other side. Cook 45 minutes to 1 hour, depending on size of chicken. Cook uncovered for crisp chicken.

CHICKEN CASSEROLE

**4 or 5 chicken breasts or
  1 whole chicken cut up
3 cans chicken soup
1 8 oz. carton sour cream
1/4 cup chicken broth
3 cylinders of Ritz crackers
1 1/2 sticks margarine (or an equal
  amount of squeeze margarine)**

Boil chicken: Save broth. Remove bones and cut chicken into bite size pieces in large pyrex dish. Mix soup, cream, and chicken broth until blended and pour over chicken. Crush crackers and pour melted or squeezed margarine over them. Coat well and put on top of chicken. Bake at 350 degrees for 30 or 35 minutes.

BAR-B-Q CHICKEN

**1 cut up chicken
1 cup Coke
1 tablespoon brown sugar
1 teaspoon salt
1 cup ketchup**

Salt chicken and place in loaf pan. Mix sugar in ketchup. Pour Coke and ketchup mixture over chicken. Bake about 1 hour at 300 degrees, or until well-done.

Taught to me by my mother Mildred Lee.

CHEESY OVEN FRIED CHICKEN

8 chicken breasts, split
1 package Ritz crackers,
  rolled to crumbs
3/4 cup parmesan cheese
1 can toasted onion rings,
  rolled to crumbs
3/4 cup butter or margarine
Salt and pepper to taste

Line large baking pan with heavy duty aluminum foil. Mix cracker crumbs, parmesan cheese, onion rings, and seasonings in a large plastic bag. Drop chicken breasts one at a time into bag until well covered and place in a single layer in baking pan. Season to taste and cover pan with foil. Bake at 325 degrees for 10 minutes and cover with melted butter. Then, continue to bake for approximately 60 minutes or until crusty and tender. Yield: 8 servings.

Goes well with yellow rice and broccoli with cheese sauce.

CHICKEN IN FOIL

6 boneless pieces of chicken breast,
  skinned
6 potatoes, sliced
1 large onion, diced
1 can Le Sueur Peas, drained
1/2 head of cabbage, shredded

Combine sliced potatoes, diced onions, shredded cabbage, and drained peas, and evenly spread over each of the six pieces of chicken. Place in 6 pieces of aluminum foil, salt and pepper to taste, and cover with foil. Wrap individually and place in large pan and cook in the oven for approximately 1 hour at 400 degrees. When done, open foil, pour into plate, and serve.

GOURMET CHINESE DISH

8 chicken breasts
2 cans Chinese noodles
2 cans cream of mushroom soup
Several green onions, chopped
Chopped almonds
1 can water chestnuts
2 cans Chinese vegetables
1 cup chopped celery
1 can milk

Grease casserole dish. Mix soup, vegetables, celery, onion, water chestnuts, almonds, milk, and 1 can Chinese noodles. Layer chicken, pour mixture over chicken. Put 1 can Chinese noodles over these layers. (This makes a large dish. May use half recipe.) Bake at 350 degrees for 2 hours (1 1/2 hours covered and last 1/2 hour uncovered).

Taught to me by my sister-in-law Vi Whitlatch.

HOT TURKEY STIR-FRY

3/4 cup water
1/3 cup red wine vinegar
1 tablespoon soy sauce
2 tablespoons cornstarch
2 teaspoons brown sugar
1/4 teaspoon garlic powder
1 cup diagonally-sliced celery
1 cup sliced fresh mushrooms
1/2 cup thin onion wedges
3 cups cooked turkey or
   chicken cut in strips
1/4 cup vegetable oil
1 teaspoon curry powder

Combine water, vinegar, soy sauce, cornstarch, brown sugar, and garlic powder; set aside. Prepare all vegetables and turkey strips before starting to cook. Heat oil in wok or large skillet. Add celery, mushrooms, and onion and stir-fry until thoroughly heated. Add turkey and curry powder and mix with vegetables. Add liquid mixture and bring to a boil. Cook stirring until mixture has boiled thoroughly and sauce clears and thickens. Serve over rice.

Makes 4 to 6 servings. Per serving: 285 calories, 16 grams fat, 405 milligrams sodium.

CORNISH GAME HENS

Prepare 6-1 lb. cornish hens for baking. Combine 1 cup orange marmalade with 2 tablespoons burgundy. Spread this on the cornish hens and bake at 375 degrees for 1 hour. Baste with marmalade mixture several times while baking. Serve with Dutch Fruit Dressing (below).

DUTCH FRUIT DRESSING

Melt 1/2 cup butter or margarine in a large skillet and sauté 1 cup chopped onions and 2 cups chopped celery until clear-looking. In a large bowl, slightly beat 2 eggs and 3 cups chicken bouillon. Add 2 cups halved grapes; 1 cup chopped apples; 1 cup cooked, pitted prunes; the celery and onions; and 1 14 oz. package of any brand seasoned dressing. Bake at 375 degrees, 30 or 40 minutes.

Taught to me by my sister-in-law Vi Whitlatch.

CREAM TUNA

2 cans white tuna
1 can Le Sueur Peas
3 hard-boiled eggs, chopped

Make a skillet of white milk gravy, add white tuna, peas, and eggs. Mix together well, salt and pepper to taste, and pour over white toast. Serves 8.

I asked my mother-in-law why and how she learned to cook this. She told me it was amazing how many kids she could feed with this because of the gravy. I can understand that! She served it years ago on biscuits as well as sandwich bread.

SALMON PATTIES

1 can red salmon
2 eggs
1 onion, diced
1 teaspoon black pepper
1/2 cup flour
1/2 cup cornmeal

Mix ingredients together and spoon into frying pan with hot oil. Fry on both sides until golden brown. Remove from heat and place on paper towel to absorb excess oil.

SALMON LOAF

1 can of red or pink salmon
1/2 cup self-rising cornmeal
1/2 cup self-rising flour
2 teaspoons dry mustard
2 eggs
1 teaspoon black pepper
1/4 cup diced onion
1 can cream of mushroom soup

Combine all ingredients and bake in a greased ovenproof dish approximately 30-40 minutes at 350 degrees.

Meats

RED AND GREEN PEPPER STEAK

1 can stewed tomatoes
2 lbs. round steak (tenderized)
1 large green bell pepper
salt and pepper to taste
1 large red bell pepper
2 medium-size banana peppers
1 large onion, diced

Cut round steak into strips approximately 1 inch wide and 4 inches long. Roll strips in flour and cook in hot cooking oil in electric skillet, browning both sides. When brown, reduce heat to medium and place bell peppers, banana peppers, and onions in skillet. Brown peppers and onions and drain off excess oil. Return to heat and add stewed tomatoes. Reduce heat and simmer for approximately 45 minutes. Also good served on a bed of rice.

I don't remember who gave me this recipe but, believe me, everyone I've cooked it for has gone nuts over it. It's delicious!

BRAISED SHORT RIBS WITH HORSERADISH DUMPLINGS

4 1/2 lbs. short ribs
1/2 cup chopped onion
1 teaspoon salt
1/4 teaspoon dried dill
1 cup (10 1/2 oz.) consomme
1 1/4 cups water
2 tablespoons flour
1 cup small whole carrots, drained

Brown short ribs in Dutch-oven-type utensils in small amount of oil. Remove all but about 2 tablespoons fat. Add onion, cook 5 minutes. Add salt, pepper, dill, consomme, and 1 cup water. Cover and simmer 1 1/2 hours or until meat is tender. Take meat from bones. Blend flour into remaining water and stir into gravy. Add carrots and keep hot.

DUMPLINGS

1 1/2 cups flour
2 teaspoons baking powder
1/2 teaspoon salt
1 tablespoon shortening
2 tablespoons horseradish
10 tablespoons milk

Sift together the flour, baking powder, and salt, cut in shortening. Add horseradish to milk and blend with flour mixture. Have the gravy gently boiling. Drop dumplings in so they rest on meat and carrots. Cover tightly; cook over low heat 15 minutes. Leave lid on.

GRILLED ORIENTAL RIBS

3 lbs. ribs

Marinate the ribs for about an hour in 1 cup of Worcestershire sauce and 1 cup of wine and pepper sauce.

Light grill 15 minutes prior to cooking.

Mix:

**3 tablespoons hot mustard
     mixed in 1/2 cup warm water
1 8 oz. jar of honey
1/2 cup melted butter**

Put ribs on the grill and brush lightly on both sides with cooking oil. Cook on low heat. Wait 5 minutes and throughout the next hour periodically baste the leftover marinating sauce with a brush. About every 15 minutes brush on hot mustard mixture. As desired, brush both sides of the ribs with honey using all 8 oz. of it. Serves 6.

My husband, George Richey, does a wonderful job on this dish. He grills outside in the summer. It has an Oriental flavor. He simply made his own recipe.

RIBS A-LA-GOULASH

1 large slab of country style ribs
1/2 head red cabbage
1 can stewed tomatoes
1 can of sauerkraut, drained
1/2 head green cabbage
4 teaspoons brown sugar
1 large onion, diced
Salt and pepper

Place ribs in a large deep saucepan. Slice ribs and cover with water. Cook on medium heat until tender. Reduce heat to low and add diced onion. Add cabbage and kraut and cook on low heat until some of the water cooks down. Salt and pepper to taste.

An old Itawamba County recipe.

BAKED BEANS AND WIENERS

2 cans of pork and beans
2 tablespoons mustard
2 tablespoons ketchup
3/4 cup onion, diced
1 lb. wieners
2 tablespoons brown sugar

Bring wieners to a boil in a saucepan. Remove from heat, drain and chop into slices. Combine beans, mustard, ketchup, onion, and brown sugar. Pour into ovenproof dish. Place chopped wieners on top of beans. Cover with foil and bake at 375 degrees for 30 minutes.

COUNTRY FRIED STEAK
AND GRAVY

6 slices of round steak (tenderized)

Pour 1 cup flour into a small bowl. Add 1 teaspoon salt and 1 teaspoon black pepper, mix well. Take each piece of tenderized steak and roll in the flour on both sides. Cover well with flour. Take 1 large skillet and heat 1 cup of Crisco in it. When the Crisco is hot, reduce heat to medium. Place each piece of steak into skillet and brown both sides. When steak is brown on both sides, drain off all excess grease. When grease is drained pour enough water into the skillet to completely cover all pieces of steak. When covered with water, cover with lid and reduce heat to simmer. Cook on simmer until steak is tender. The water will form a gravy.

Being born and raised on a farm, I didn't know there was any other kind of steak than country fried until after I was married. We raised our hogs, chicken, and cattle and my grandfather had a brother who was a marksman with the rifle. We slaughtered our own. All I had to hear was "Send Claud after his rifle." I hid in a closet until it was all over. That's one of the few bad memories I have of the farm.

SHEPHERD'S PIE

**2 lb. meat (lamb or beef),
    boned and cubed
2 tablespoons flour
Salt and pepper
1/4 teaspoon chili powder
3 tablespoons vegetable oil**

Wipe meat with damp cloth. Mix flour, salt, pepper, and chili powder and roll meat in this mixture. Brown well in hot oil. Pour off excess oil.

**2 8 oz. cans tomato sauce
2 cups water
Salt
1 bay leaf
8 small onions
1/2 lb. string beans (fresh or canned)
4 carrots, quartered**

Mix tomato sauce, water, salt, and bay leaf. Pour over meat and simmer covered for 1 1/4 hours. Add vegetables and cook 30 minutes longer. Pour stew into 2 quart casserole and top with 2 cups mashed potatoes arranged around outside of casserole dish. Bake at 375 degrees about 15 minutes.

This is a dish from London, England. I prefer beef, but you can use lamb or both if you like. I learned to eat it when I couldn't find good country food over there.

HUSBAND'S DELIGHT

1 lb. ground beef
1 teaspoon garlic salt
1/2 teaspoon black pepper
1 teaspoon salt
2 small cans of tomato sauce
1 package (small) noodles
1 carton sour cream
5 small green onions or
**   1/2 cup onions, chopped**
1/2 to 1 cup cheddar cheese, grated

Brown meat with seasoning. Drain beef. Add tomato sauce. Cover and simmer for 15 minutes. Cook noodles and drain. Mix sour cream and onions. Butter casserole dish and layer ingredients in the following order: Noodles, beef mixture and sour cream mixture. Sprinkle cheese on top and bake in 325-degree oven for 20 minutes. (Suitable for freezing.)

This is another dish I'd prepare before leaving on a long tour. I would leave this frozen for the children to eat while I was gone. Good for a husband to take out frozen and serve. Sure makes daddy look good!

COUNTRY STYLE RIB STEW

**2 packages country style pork ribs
(split backbone) browned in oven**

Add:

**1 number 2 can kraut and
1 small can, drained
2 cans stewed tomatoes
1 medium size cabbage
1/4 cup brown sugar
Salt and pepper to taste**

Add water, cook in pot at low temperature for 2 hours.

*This was given to me by my dearest friend, Maxine Hyder,
when we lived in Lakeland, Florida. She taught me so very
many different and tasty recipes, along with many ways to
cook an ordinary dish.*

BRISKET OF BEEF

Marinate 5 to 7 lbs. beef brisket in 1/2 bottle of liquid smoke, salt
and pepper overnight. Next morning, cover brisket with paprika,
celery salt, garlic salt, (sprinkle with dry onion soup mix), sliced
onions, and nutmeg. 1 cup Bar-B-Que sauce, 1/2 cup water.
Bake at 325 degrees for 5 to 6 hours. Last hour, pour 12 oz. can
of beer and continue baking. Cool and slice.

DE-LIS-CIOUS!

Taught to me by my sister-in-law Vi Whitlatch.

CHILI

2 lbs. ground beef
4 tablespoons chili powder
1 package of chili seasoning
2 medium onions, diced
2 8-oz. cans tomato sauce
1 pint water
2 cans chili beans
1/4 cup sugar

Mix ground beef, chili powder, chili seasoning, and onions and brown in skillet. Drain off excess fat. Add tomato sauce, water, beans, and sugar. Simmer approximately 40 minutes.

If you like your chili hot, add 2 small jalapeño peppers while simmering.

QUICHE WITHOUT A CRUST

1 lb. sausage, fried and drained
3 slices cubed, brown bread
1 cup grated cheddar cheese
6 eggs
2 cups milk
1 teaspoon salt
1 teaspoon dry mustard

Layer bread, sausage, and cheese. Cover with mixture of remaining ingredients. Refrigerate 24 hours. Let stand at room temperature before baking 45 minutes at 350 degrees.

STEW

With this recipe you can use ground beef or stew meat.

1 lb. ground beef or stew meat
6 quartered potatoes
1/2 cup diced celery
1/4 cup sugar
2 cans stewed tomatoes
4 chopped carrots
1 diced onion
Salt and pepper to taste

Combine all ingredients in deep stewer. Cover and cook on medium until tender and desired thickness.

STUFFED PORK CHOPS

6 pork chops (cut 1/2 inches thick
with a pocket cut on the side)

Roll pork shops in flour on both sides before frying, then fry pork chops in a large skillet with about 1/2 inch of cooking oil. (While oil is hot put pork chops in.) Salt and pepper to taste. Fry on each side until brown then remove and let cool.

Use cornbread dressing recipe cut in half for your stuffing. When dressing is ready stuff into the pockets on the sides of the pork chops. Place stuffed chops into an ovenproof dish (buttered). Any dressing left over, scatter around the pork chops and bake at 350 degrees until tender and brown.

CANE BAY GLAZED PORK LOIN

1 4 to 5 lb. pork loin
1/2 teaspoon pepper
1 6oz. can frozen orange juice
  (thawed)
1 teaspoon dry mustard
3 drops Tabasco sauce
Salt
3/4 teaspoon garlic powder
1/2 cup dark molasses
1/2 cup apricot preserves
1/4 teaspoon ground cloves

Sprinkle loin with salt, pepper, and 1/2 teaspoon garlic powder. Crisscross fat of loin with knife. Place loin on rack in foil-lined pan.

Combine 1/4 teaspoon salt, 1/4 teaspoon garlic powder, and all remaining ingredients.

Brush loin with glaze. Preheat oven to 350 degrees and cook about 30 minutes per pound. Brush with glaze every 15 minutes.

Taught to me by my sister-in-law Marie Meier.

MEXICAN MEAT LOAF

1 1/2 lbs. ground beef
1/2 cup uncooked oats
1/2 onion, diced
1/4 cup Worcestershire sauce
1 4 oz. can green chilis, diced
4 oz. cream cheese
8 oz. salsa

Combine ground beef with oats, onion, and Worcestershire. Mix well. Press the mixture approximately 1 inch thick on wax paper.

Mix green chilis and cream cheese. Spread on top of ground beef and roll into cylinder shape. Place into greased ovenproof dish. Cook approximately 30 minutes at 350 degrees. Remove and cover with 8 oz. salsa. Return to stove and cook 7-10 minutes. Remove and serve.

SLOPPY JOES

1 lb. ground beef
1 cup diced onion
1/2 bell pepper, diced
1 small can tomato paste
1 small can tomato sauce
2 tablespoons brown sugar

Brown beef, onion, and bell pepper in small amount of cooking oil in frying pan. When browned, drain off excess grease. Add brown sugar, salt and pepper to taste. Add tomato sauce and tomato paste. Simmer approximately 30 minutes, stirring occasionally. Serve on top of warm buns.

FAMILY SWISS STEAK

1 1/2 - 2 lb. round steak 1 inch thick
1/3 cup flour
1 1/2 teaspoons salt
1/8 teaspoon pepper
3 tablespoons oil
1 8oz. can tomato sauce
1/2 cup water
1 teaspoon Worcestershire sauce
Bay leaf
2 medium onions, sliced
1 green pepper, cut in rings
2 tablespoons sugar

Combine flour, salt, and pepper. Pound mixture into meat with edge of saucer until flour is used up. Brown meat in oil. Add tomato sauce, water, Worcestershire sauce, bay leaf, and sugar. Cover and simmer 1 hour. Add onions and green pepper, cover, and cook 30 minutes longer or until tender. Serve over cooked noodles or rice.

Taught to me by Bonnie Wilson.

E-Z CORN DOGS

1 cup pancake mix
2 tablespoons cornmeal
1 tablespoon sugar
2/3 cup water
1 package wieners
Cooking oil
Corn dog sticks

Heat cooking oil in deep narrow pan (or coffee can works very well for this). Mix together pancake mix, cornmeal, sugar, and water. Pour batter in a tall glass. Wipe wieners off well with a paper towel. Push stick into each wiener and dip it into the batter until well coated. Hold in hot cooking oil until golden brown. Makes 8.

GROUND BEEF, CHEESE, AND POTATO CASSEROLE

1 onion, diced
6 medium-size potatoes, quartered
1 lb. ground beef
8 slices American cheese
salt & pepper to taste

Cook six quartered potatoes in a saucepan until tender. Drain off water and pour potatoes into an ovenproof buttered pan.

Place ground beef in skillet with diced onion and brown. Remove from skillet, drain, and pour on top of potatoes in the ovenproof dish. Place cheese slices on top of ground beef. Place in oven on 350 degrees and cook until all cheese slices have melted. Serve hot.

CROCKPOT POT ROAST

3-4 lbs. rump roast or pot roast
2-4 potatoes, pared and sliced
1-4 carrots, pared and sliced
1-2 onions, pared and sliced
1 clove garlic, chopped
Salt and pepper to taste

Put onion in bottom of crockpot. Salt and pepper meat, then put in pot. Add liquid (small amount of water to prevent sticking). Put vegetables on top, cover and cook on low for 10-12 hours. (4-5 hours on high.)

Taught to me by my mother Mildred Lee.

HO BO DINNERS

With this recipe you can use pork chops, chicken, hamburger meat, or small steaks.

INGREDIENTS:
Cabbage
Potatoes
Celery
Carrots
Squash
Le Sueur peas
Onion
Zucchini

Salt and pepper to taste. Wine and pepper sauce 4 tablespoons per serving. Worcestershire sauce 4 tablespoons per serving. Butter 4 tablespoons per serving.

Dice vegetables in large bowl. Combine all ingredients and divide evenly. Place portions on pieces of aluminum foil about 18″ x 18″ . Place meat on top of vegetables. Add wine and pepper sauce, Worcestershire sauce, and butter. Fold foil securely to prevent any leakage. Place on grill and cook for approximately 45 minutes. When cooked, drain off any excess liquid. This is a complete meal.

Taught to me by my husband George Richey.

BAKED HAM

**1 small fresh ham or
1 2 lb. canned ham**

MIX:

**1/2 cup honey
4 tablespoons mustard
2 teaspoons sesame seeds**

Pour 1/2 of the mixture on ham and bake in 350 degree oven for approximately 40 minutes. Remove from oven and pour on remainder of glaze. Return to oven and bake until ham is tender throughout. A fresh ham takes a couple of hours. A canned ham will take less time.

Vegetables

SQUASH PUPPIES

2 cups self-rising cornmeal
1 1/2 cups squash
1 large onion
1/2 teaspoon salt
1 cup self-rising flour
1 cup buttermilk
2 eggs
1/4 teaspoon pepper

Boil squash until tender, drain. Mash squash, add onion and eggs. Mix dry ingredients and add to squash mixture. Add buttermilk (beer optional), mix. Let set 1 hour before cooking. Cook in deep-fat cooker for 2 to 3 minutes until brown.

POLK SALAD AND EGGS

Buy fresh polk salad or pick your own. Wash thoroughly and place in deep cooking stewer. Cover with water and let cook for approximately 25 minutes. Remove from heat and pour off all water since polk salad is poisonous unless this is done. Return to stewer, cover with water and par boil over again for approximately 20 minutes. Remove from heat again and drain well. Set aside. In a skillet put 1/2 cup cooking oil and add 1 diced onion. Brown onion. Pour the drained polk salad into skillet and add 6 beaten eggs. Cook on medium heat until dry. (Good country meal!)

> *My stepfather, Peepaw, would begin picking this as soon as it sprouted in the spring. He taught me what to look for. When it got big and tall and we went to seed it, it had red berries on it that stained very badly. My school friends and I used to use this to paint our lips and cheeks.*

SPINACH PIE

1 can spinach (or fresh if desired),
  cooked and drained
4 eggs
1/2 cup Monterey Jack cheese
1/2 cup cheddar cheese, shredded
1/2 cup heavy whipping cream
1/2 cup fresh bacon bits
1 9-inch pie shell

Add spinach with eggs, stir in cheese, the whipping cream and the bacon bits. Mix together and pour mixture into 9″ uncooked pie shell. Preheat oven to 350 degrees. Place pie in oven and cook until firm. Use toothpick to check. If toothpick comes out clean, pie is done. Cool and slice.

> *I was in California doing a country music award show and the hotel I was staying at served this dish. I asked for the recipe and they gave it to me. Good hot or cold. I have given this recipe to many people.*

CORNMEAL FRIED POTATOES

Peel 8 medium-size white Irish potatoes. Slice across the potatoes. Pour 1 cup of self-rising cornmeal into a small bowl. Roll each slice of potato in the cornmeal, covering each slice evenly and heavy. Pour 3/4 cup cooking oil into large frying pan. Drop each slice of potato into hot oil. Cook on medium heat and brown on both sides. Drain all excess oil and turn heat to simmer. Pour enough regular milk into frying pan to completely cover all potato slices. Salt and pepper to taste. Cover and cook on simmer until milk has thickened into gravy. Serve hot.

> *There must be 101 ways to cook potatoes, so here is number 102. It's unusual and very good.*

Above: Onstage in England with my godchild.

At Left: With my husband, George Richey. (Photograph by Einstein Photo)

Above: Preparing a meal with friends.

CANDIED YAMS

Combine 2 cups cooked, mashed sweet potatoes with 2/3 cup brown sugar, 1/4 cup melted margarine or butter, 1/2 cup orange juice, 1 teaspoon pumpkin pie spice, 1/4 cup chopped nuts, and 1/2 cup raisins (optional). Place slices of pineapple (20 oz. can) in a baking dish. Put approximately 1/3 cup of the yam mixture on top of each slice of pineapple. Bake at 375 degrees for 20 minutes. Top with miniature marshmallows and bake about 5 minutes longer.

Taught to me by my sister-in-law Vi Whitlatch.

CHEESE POTATOES

Cut 6-8 medium-size potatoes into quarters. Place into deep saucepan. Cover with water and cook until potatoes are tender. Add salt and pepper to taste. When potatoes are tender, drain off all water. Turn heat to low or simmer. Pour enough milk to completely cover the potatoes. Add 10 slices of American cheese. Cook until thick on low heat. (You may want to add more black pepper.)

This is my daughter Gwen's favorite. She doesn't cook very much but she has called home from Colorado asking for this recipe. Even her husband Charlie likes it.

FRIED SWEET POTATOES

Slice 4-6 medium-size fresh sweet potatoes. Put 1 stick of butter into frying pan and melt. Place sliced potatoes in frying pan on medium heat and fry until tender, turning frequently. Sprinkle with 1/2 cup brown sugar while frying. Remove from pan, place on paper towel to absorb the butter then put on plate and serve.

SQUASH CASSEROLE (1)

3 cups cooked squash
2 eggs
1 teaspoon black pepper
1 cup evaporated milk
3/4 cup chopped onions
1 cup grated cheese
2 cups cracker crumbs
3/4 stick of butter

Cook squash. Drain off the water. Add melted butter, salt, pepper, and milk to squash. Then add beaten eggs and cheese. Add onions.

Mix cracker crumbs with melted butter and sprinkle on top of casserole. Bake at 325 degrees for 45 minutes.

Taught to me by my mother Mildred Lee.

SQUASH CASSEROLE (2)

**2 cups Pepperidge Farm
  Herb Stuffing
2 cups summer squash,
  cleaned and sliced thin
1 small container sour cream
1 medium onion, chopped
1 stick butter or margarine
1 can cream of chicken soup
1 or 2 carrots, grated
Salt and pepper to taste**

Slice squash and place in saucepan with small amount of water. Cook about 3 minutes until slightly tender. Drain well.

Grate carrots and onion. Add to cooked squash. Mix sour cream and soup well and add to the above mixture. Salt and pepper. Set aside.

Melt one stick butter and add to herb stuffing. Mix well. Line casserole dish with half of stuffing mixture. Add squash mixture. Top with remaining bread crumb topping. Bake at 375 degrees for 45 minutes.

Taught to me by my sister-in-law Marie Meier. People that like this casserole say they don't like squash.

BROCCOLI SOUFFLÉ

**2 packages frozen broccoli,
  cooked and drained
1 can cream of mushroom soup
1 cup cheddar cheese, grated
2 beaten eggs.
1 small onion, chopped
1 cup mayonnaise
Ritz cracker crumbs and margarine**

Mix soup, mayonnaise, eggs, onion, and cheese together. Put broccoli in casserole dish and add the soup mixture. Sprinkle Ritz cracker crumbs and margarine on top. Bake at 350 degrees for 45 minutes.

Taught to me by my sister-in-law Vi Whitlatch.

BROCCOLI AND RICE
CASSEROLE

**1 can cream of chicken soup
1 small jar of Cheez-Whiz
2 packages chopped broccoli
2 cups cooked rice**

Cook broccoli as directed and drained. Cook rice. Layer rice and broccoli, beginning with rice. Mix undiluted chicken soup with Cheez-Whiz and beat until blended. Pour over layers. Take a fork and wiggle it through the layers.

Taught to me by Gerald & Sandra Jetton.

MISSISSIPPI-STYLE
STUFFED BELL PEPPERS

**1 pan cooked cornbread
(8 x 12-inch pan)
1 16-oz. can Le Sueur peas, drained
6 large bell peppers, cored, parboiled
1 16-oz. can niblet corn, drained
1 16-oz. can stewed tomatoes,
chopped
1-2 pounds canned ham, cut into
1-inch squares
6 strips of bacon**

Preheat oven to 300 degrees. Crumble cornbread into large mixing bowl. Add corn, tomatoes, and peas. Mix until evenly moist. Add ham and mix thoroughly. Stuff peppers with mixture from the bowl. Stuff excess stuffing around peppers and place one strip of bacon on top of each pepper. Bake for 40 minutes.

Makes 6 servings.

I've never known anyone to make stuffed peppers like this. My grandmother, Flora Russell, made this as far back as I can remember. It's a very different dish.

BROWN RICE

1 can beef consommé
1 can onion soup
1 cup long grain rice
1 stick butter
1/2 cup water
1 large jar mushrooms

Melt butter in casserole dish and add the above ingredients. Bake at 325 degrees for 1 hour.

BAKED TOMATO

2 fresh tomatoes
1 clove garlic, minced
1/4 teaspoon tarragon
1/4 teaspoon basil
Fresh-ground pepper, to taste
1 tablespoon Parmesan cheese

Slice tomatoes in half. Place in shallow baking pan, flat side up. Combine the seasonings and cheese and sprinkle over tomatoes. Bake at 350 degrees for about 30 minutes or until tender. Makes 4 servings at about 28 calories per serving.

CORNFLAKE POTATOES

4 medium sweet potatoes, cooked
1/4 cup squeeze butter
1/2 cup chopped nuts
 (walnuts, pecans, etc.)
1/2 cup coconut
3/4 cup brown sugar

Mix all ingredients.

1 cup frosted flakes
4 tablespoons squeeze butter
1/2 cup brown sugar

Mix all ingredients. Place on top of sweet potatoes and bake at 350 degrees until bubbly.

POTATO PATTIES

3 cups leftover mashed potatoes
1 egg
1/4 cup cornmeal
1/2 cup flour
1/2 cup diced onion
1 teaspoon black pepper

Combine leftover potatoes with egg, onion, black pepper, flour, and cornmeal. Shape into patties. Fry in butter in skillet until golden brown on both sides.

POTATO CASSEROLE

**1 32-oz. package frozen
hash brown potatoes**
2 cans cream of chicken soup
1 1/3 cups grated cheese
1/4 teaspoon pepper
1/2 cup melted butter
1 carton sour cream
1/2 cup onions, chopped
1 teaspoon salt

Mix all very well and put in buttered casserole dish.

TOPPING

1/4 cup butter
2 cups Corn Flake crumbs

Bake at 350 degrees for 1 hour.

Taught to me by my sister-in-law Vi Whitlatch.

FRIED OKRA AND
GREEN TOMATOES

2 lbs. sliced okra
4 green tomatoes, sliced
1 cup diced onion
2 banana peppers

Cut up okra, green tomatoes, and peppers. Roll in self-rising cornmeal. Put small amount of cooking oil in skillet and cook over medium-low heat, turning until browned. Cover and simmer a few minutes.

OKRA AND TOMATOES

2 lbs. okra
2 stalks celery
1 cup diced onion
6 fresh tomatoes or
    2 small cans of stewed tomatoes
Salt and pepper

Cut and fry okra in skillet with 4 tablespoons of cooking oil. Add onion and celery and cook until slightly brown. Remove from heat and drain off excess grease. Return to heat and add tomatoes, salt and pepper to taste. Simmer for approximately 40 minutes. (This recipe is very good served on a bed of rice.)

FRIED GREEN TOMATOES

1 cup self-rising cornmeal
6 medium-size green tomatoes,
  sliced
1/2 cup hot oil
Salt and pepper

Pour self-rising cornmeal into a small bowl. Slice the green tomatoes approximately 1/4 inch thick. Roll each slice in cornmeal. Cook in skillet on medium temperature with hot oil. Brown evenly on both sides. Salt and pepper to taste.

OKRA FRITTERS

1 cup thinly-sliced okra
1/2 cup chopped tomato
1/2 cup chopped onion
1/4 teaspoon pepper
1/4 cup Bisquick
1/4 cup cornmeal
1/2 teaspoon salt
1/2 teaspoon curry powder
1 egg, beaten

Combine all ingredients, stirring well. Drop by tablespoonful into hot oil, cooking till golden brown, turning once.

Note: If you add another egg and slightly more flour or Bisquick, you have a good meatless main dish.

You can also slice the okra and chop the tomatoes and freeze in Seal-a-Meal or Ziploc bags for use in winter months.

COUNTRY PEAS AND OKRA

This recipe can be used with canned peas or fresh.

Pour canned peas into a saucepan. Put a thick layer of fresh, whole okra (washed) on top of the peas. Cover with water. Add 1/2 cup of cooking oil, salt and pepper. Add 2 or 3 slices of salt pork. Cover and cook on medium heat until okra is tender. If using fresh peas, cook the peas for at least 30-40 minutes before adding the okra.

SPICY BAKED BEANS

1 lb. ground beef
1 bell pepper
1 medium onion, chopped
1 cup celery, chopped
1/4 cup chili powder
2 16-oz. cans Van Camp beans
1/2 cup brown sugar
1 cup ketchup

Cook first five ingredients in pan. Mix beans, sugar, and ketchup. Combine everything and mix well. Bake at 350 degrees approximately 50 minutes.

Taught to me by Fae Crane.

LIMA BEAN BAKE

1/2 lb. bacon, cut in 3 strips
1 medium onion, chopped
1/2 cup bell pepper, chopped
4 cans (#2) lima beans,
    drained and rinsed
3/4 bottle ketchup
2 cans tomato soup
2 cups brown sugar

Mix all ingredients together and place in glass baking dish. Bake at 350 degrees for 1 1/2 to 2 hours.

Taught to me by my sister-in-law Marie Meier.

FRIED MUSHROOMS

1 egg, separated
1/2 cup beer
Tabasco sauce
1/2 cup and 2 tablespoons
    sifted flour
1/2 teaspoon salt
1/2 teaspoon paprika
1 tablespoon melted butter

Beat egg yolk with beer and a dash of Tabasco. Add flour, salt, paprika and stir until batter is smooth. Stir in melted butter. Beat egg white until stiff and fluffy and gently fold in egg white. Dip mushrooms in batter and fry.

Taught to me by my niece Lisa Meier Hadden.

FRESH FRIED CORN

1/4 cup sugar
8 ears of fresh corn
1/4 cup self-rising flour
1/2 cup water
Salt and pepper

With a sharp knife cut the tips of the corn off holding the corn inside a bowl and using a downward stroke. When all the kernels have been cut off, using the knife, scrape the remainder of the kernels off into the same bowl.

Place cut off corn into large skillet with about 1/2 cup of cooking oil. Add 1/4 cup of sugar and enough water to make the mixture thin. Mix 1/4 cup of self-rising flour into 1/2 cup water. Stir this mixture into the corn. Cook on medium heat until desired thickness. Add salt and pepper to taste.

HOMINY CASSEROLE

1 stick margarine
1/2 cup celery, diced
1/2 cup onion, diced
1 can mushroom soup
1 large can hominy (or 2 small cans)
1 bell pepper, diced
1 cup grated cheese

Sauté the onion, celery, and bell pepper in margarine. Add 1 can mushroom soup and hominy. Place in ungreased casserole dish. Bake until bubbly. Remove and add grated cheese. Place back in oven and lightly brown.

SKILLET FRIED CABBAGE

1 medium-size head of cabbage
1 cup diced onion
1 teaspoon black pepper
Salt
6 tablespoons cooking oil

Melt 6 tablespoons cooking oil in skillet. Place into skillet, coarsely-cut cabbage and onion. Pour one cup of water. Cook on medium heat until cabbage is tender. Salt to taste.

SWEET AND SOUR CUCUMBERS

1/2 cup white vinegar
1/3 cup salad oil
2 tablespoons sugar
1 teaspoon salt
1/4 teaspoon white pepper
1/4 teaspoon oregano leaves
3 medium cucumbers, peeled and
thinly sliced

About an hour before serving or up to 2 days ahead, combine all ingredients, cover and refrigerate. Stir occasionally.

Taught to me by Jane Williams.

EASY SWEET, WHOLE CUCUMBER PICKLES

Buy 1 gallon jar of whole sour pickles (not dill). Drain all liquid from pickles. Slice thin on paper towels. Pat the slices to remove as much liquid as possible. Take five pounds sugar and alternate layers of pickles and sugar (no liquid). You may have to wait awhile before you can get them all in jar (they will settle down). Shake occasionally until sugar melts. These are crispy and delicious. They DO NOT have to be refrigerated.

CUCUMBER AND ONIONS

Peel two medium-size onions. Pull the onions apart in rings.

Slice three medium-sized cucumbers (peeled). Place onion rings in a bowl with sliced cucumbers. Add 1 cup of sour cream and mix well. Chill and serve.

FRESH TURNIP GREENS

The amount of turnip greens you use does not really matter. Just keep in mind that if your pot is completely full when you start cooking, they will cook down to about 1/2 of the full amount.

Place your greens in a deep pot and cover with water. Quarter six turnips and cook with the greens. Add 4 slices of salt pork, 1/2 cup cooking oil, cover with water and cook slowly until tender. Salt to taste.

ASPARAGUS CASSEROLE

2 cans asparagus spears
1/2 can cream of mushroom soup
1/4 to 1/2 cup grated processed
 cheese or Cheez-Whiz spread
3 hard-boiled eggs, sliced
1 pimiento, chopped
Cracker crumbs

CHEESE SAUCE

2 tablespoons fat
1 1/4 cups asparagus stock
4 tablespoons flour
1/2 cup sweet milk

Melt fat in skillet, add flour, and blend. Add liquid and cook over low heat. Add cheese and soup, stirring constantly, until desired consistency. Alternate ingredients in layers in a well-greased casserole dish. Top with remainder of crumbs and with butter. Bake in moderate oven until well heated.

SPICED CARROTS

**1 lb. carrots, cooked
  (sliced diagonally)
2 cups tomato juice;
  cook until one cup remains**

Add to juice:

**1/2 cup vinegar
2 teaspoons prepared mustard
1 cup sugar
1 1/2 teaspoons salt**

Pour over carrots and simmer 5 minutes. Marinate 24 hours. Serve hot or cold.

Taught to me by my niece Brenda Kennedy.

SPINACH SOUFFLÉ

**2 10-oz. packages chopped spinach,
  cooked and drained
4 eggs, slightly beaten
2/3 cup milk
2 teaspoons salt
2 cups cooked rice
2 cups grated cheddar cheese
4 tablespoons butter
1 teaspoon Worcestershire sauce
1/2 teaspoon rosemary and thyme**

Mix well and bake at 350 degrees for 20 to 25 minutes.

Taught to me by my sister-in-law Vi Whitlatch.

SAUSAGE CABBAGE CASSEROLE

1 medium size head of cabbage
1 10 oz. package sausage links
1 can condensed tomato soup
2 cups milk
1 can cream of chicken soup
1 cup diced onion
1/4 cup flour

Rinse cabbage, slice, and put into saucepan. Add chicken soup. Cover and boil 5 minutes then drain. In greased frying pan, cook sausage links for about 6 minutes. Remove from pan. After removing sausage, place onion in same pan and fry for 5 minutes. Add tomato soup and stir in flour. Gradually add milk. Cook slowly until thickened. In a buttered large casserole dish, alternate layers of cabbage and sauce. Place sausage links on top. Bake at 325 degrees for 25 minutes.

SWEET POTATO CASSEROLE (1)

3 cups baked sweet potatoes
  (mash well)
2 eggs
1 teaspoon vanilla
1/3 cup evaporated (Pet or
  Eagle brand) milk
1 cup sugar
1/2 cup butter or margarine

Place in glass baking dish.

TOPPING

1 cup brown sugar
1/3 cup butter or margarine
1/2 cup flour
1 cup walnuts

Mix and sprinkle over potatoes. Bake at 375 degrees approximately 30 minutes.

Taught to me by my sister-in-law Marie Meier.

SWEET POTATO CASSEROLE (2)

Peel and boil enough sweet potatoes to make 3 or 4 cups mashed. Whip with beater. Mix with 1 stick oleo, 1/2 cup sugar, 2 eggs, 1 cup evaporated milk (I use Eagle Brand), and 1 teaspoon vanilla. Beat with mixer, and pour in casserole dish.

TOPPING

Melt 1 stick margarine, add 1/2 cup brown sugar, 1/2 cup pecans, and 1 cup crushed cornflake crumbs (or Rice Krispies). Put on top of potatoes and bake about 45 minutes at 325-350 degrees.

Taught to me by my mother Mildred Lee.

STIR-FRIED RATATOUILLE

6 tablespoons oil
2 teaspoons Italian seasoning
1/4 teaspoon pepper
1 medium eggplant, peeled and cut
    into 1/2 inch cubes
Italian cheese (parmesan or
    romano), grated
2 teaspoons parsley flakes
1 teaspoon salt
Two 6-8-inch zucchini,
    quartered lengthwise and cubed
1 medium red onion, chopped
1 large sweet pepper, chopped
3 or 4 medium tomatoes, quartered

Heat oil with next four ingredients until very hot in wok or very large iron skillet. Add eggplant and zucchini. Stir fry until half cooked (do not let it brown). Add chopped onion and peppers. Continue to stir until crisp, cooked. Add tomatoes and continue to stir until tomatoes are just hot through. Sprinkle parsley flakes on top after cooking. Put in serving dish and sprinkle with grated Italian cheese. Serves 6 to 8.

Note: Stir fried vegetables should never be overcooked; just to crisp, tender stage.

HOW TO MAKE CANNED VEGETABLES
TASTE HOMEMADE

1. **GREEN BEANS:**
   Drain off all water, place beans in saucepan, and add fresh water. Dice 1 small onion, add 1/4 cup cooking oil, 3 slices of salt pork, and salt and pepper to taste. Cook until salt pork is tender. The same recipe applies to pinto beans or canned lima beans. Add 1 teaspoon of sugar.

2. **SAUERKRAUT:**
   Drain off all water and replace with fresh water. Add 1/4 cup cooking oil and cook approximately 15 minutes. Same applies to hominy except use butter instead of cooking oil.

3. **CORN (Niblet style):**
   Drain off all water and replace with fresh water. Add 3 tablespoons of flour mixed in a cup with 1/2 cup of milk. Add 1/2 teaspoon of black pepper. This thickens the corn. If it is too thick, simply add more water. Add 1 teaspoon sugar and salt and pepper to taste.

4. **PEAS (all except sweet green peas):**
   Drain off all water, adding fresh water. Add 1/4 cup cooking oil and 1 diced onion. Cook approximately 15-20 minutes. Salt and pepper to taste.

Desserts

SOUR CREAM POUND CAKE

1 cup Crisco
3 cups sugar
6 eggs
1 carton (1 cup) sour cream
3 cups plain flour
1/2 teaspoon soda
Dash of salt
2 tablespoons coconut or
**   vanilla flavoring**

Cream sugar and Crisco. Add eggs. Blend rest of ingredients one at a time. Bake at 325 degrees 1 hour or until done.

> *Taught to me by Gerald and Sandra Jetton. Every time Gerald and Sandra come to visit or every time they meet me on the road for a show, I beg them to bring this cake. My favorite cakes are these without the frosting.*

BANANA NUT CAKE

1 cup shortening
1 cup ripe mashed bananas
3 cups flour
1/4 cup buttermilk
1 teaspoon vanilla
2 cups sugar
2 eggs, beaten
1 teaspoon soda
1 cup pecans, chopped

Cream shortening, add sugar, then bananas. Mix well and add eggs, flour, and milk alternately to banana mixture. Beat well, add nuts and vanilla last. Bake in layers or bundt pan.

RED VELVET CAKE

2 1/2 cups plain flour
3 tablespoons cocoa
2 eggs
2 1-oz. bottles red food coloring
1 cup buttermilk
1 teaspoon baking soda
1/2 teaspoon salt
1/2 cup butter
1 1/2 cups sugar
1 teaspoon vanilla
1 tablespoon white vinegar

Sift together flour, salt, and cocoa. Cream butter and sugar. When well creamed, beat in whole eggs one at a time. Blend well and add food coloring and vanilla. Mix buttermilk, vinegar, and soda. Add alternately with dry ingredients to cream mixture. Blend at low speed on electric mixer between each addition. Grease and line two 9-inch cake pans. Pour in batter and bake in preheated oven at 350 degrees about 30 minutes or until lightly browned. Don't overbake. Let cool before frosting.

ICING

4 tablespoons flour
1 cup sugar
1/2 cup shortening
1/4 teaspoon salt
1 cup sweet milk
1 stick butter
3 teaspoons vanilla

Blend flour and milk. Cook until mixture thickens to consistency of cream. Cool but don't chill. Cream sugar, butter, and shortening, adding sweet milk and vanilla. Add cooked flour mixture and beat until fluffy. Spread on cooled cake, between layers and on top and sides.

Taught to me by my mother, Mildred Lee. This is Richey's favorite cake of all the ones that my mother bakes.

CHOCOLATE RIPPLE POUND CAKE

3 tablespoons shortening
2 cups butter or margarine, softened
10 eggs
2 teaspoons vanilla extract
1/2 cup plus 1 tablespoon cocoa
3 cups sugar
4 cups sifted cake flour

Melt shortening in small saucepan. Add cocoa, stirring until smooth, and set aside. Cream butter and gradually add sugar, beating well. Add eggs, one at a time, beating well after each addition. Add flour and vanilla, mixing well. Remove 2 cups of batter and add chocolate mixture, stirring until blended. Spoon 1/3 remaining batter into greased and floured 10-inch tube pan, and top with 1/2 of chocolate batter. Repeat layers ending with plain batter. Draw a knife through batter to make a swirl design. Bake in 325-degree oven for 1 hour and 30 minutes or until a wooden toothpick comes out clean. Cool cake in pan 10 minutes, remove from pan, and cool completely on a wire rack. Yield one 10-inch cake.

WHIPPING CREAM POUND CAKE

1/2 lb. real butter
6 eggs
1/2 pint whipping cream
   (do not whip)
2 tablespoons vanilla
3 cups sugar
3 cups sifted cake flour (sift twice
   or use 3 cups plain flour minus
   6 tablespoons)

Cream butter and sugar together until it reaches consistency of snow. Add egg one at a time to above mixture, beating well after each addition. Add flour and whipping cream alternately to above mixture, beating while adding (add flour first and last). Add vanilla last. Mix well. Bake in greased and floured tube pan for one hour and 15 minutes on 325 degrees. Start in cold oven!

CARAMEL ICING

2 cups sugar
3/4 cup sugar to brown
1 cup Pet milk
1/2 stick oleo

Cook 2 cups sugar and Pet milk in heavy saucepan on low heat. Caramelize 3/4 cup sugar in heavy saucepan. Add 1/2 stick oleo to caramelized sugar and stir fast while pouring milk mixture into it. Cook to soft ball stage. Remove from heat and beat to consistency to spread on cake.

OLD FASHIONED TEA CAKES
(My favorites)

1 1/2 cups margarine
3 eggs, beaten thoroughly
2 cups sugar
1 tablespoon vanilla
1 tablespoon powder
4 cups self-rising flour

Soften margarine to room temperature. Beat in eggs, sugar, and vanilla. Add baking powder to flour and sift together, slowly, into margarine mixture. Roll out on floured board and cut with cookie cutter. Bake in preheated oven at 350 degrees until as brown as desired.

Makes 5-6 dozen.

ANGEL FOOD CAKE
(EXTRA LARGE)

1 pint cake flour
1 1/4 pints sugar
1 pint egg whites
1 1/4 teaspoons cream of tartar
1/4 teaspoon salt
1 teaspoon vanilla or lemon extract

Sift flour and sugar together five times. Beat egg whites until foamy, add cream of tartar and salt, beat until egg whites will hold a stiff peak. Fold flour and sugar mixture into egg whites a tablespoon at a time. Bake in a large, ungreased tube pan in moderate oven, 325 degrees, for 75 minutes. Invert pan to cool. The longer the cake remains in pan, the more brown crust adheres to pan.

FRESH APPLE CAKE

3 cups diced apples
1 2/3 cups sugar
1/2 teaspoon salt
1 teaspoon cinnamon
1/2 teaspoon allspice

Mix and let set while preparing other ingredients.

2/3 cup oil
1 1/2 teaspoons soda
2 cups flour
2 eggs

Beat eggs, add oil, sift flour with soda, add apple mixture, and mix real well. You may want to add 1 cup chopped nuts. Bake at 325 degrees for 45 to 60 minutes. Serve warm with English toffee ice cream or lemon glaze.

LEMON GLAZE

1 cup powdered sugar
1 tablespoon white syrup
1 1/2 tablespoons lemon juice
1/2 teaspoon vanilla

Taught to me by my sister-in-law Vi Whitlatch. Vi and her husband Bill lived with us for a while and helped take care of the children. She also cooked for us.

GREAT CHOCOLATE CAKE

2 cups sugar
1/2 cup shortening
1 cup water
1/2 cup buttermilk
1 teaspoon soda
1 teaspoon cinnamon
2 cups flour
1 stick butter or margarine
4 tablespoons cocoa
2 eggs, beaten
1 teaspoon vanilla

Sift together sugar and flour. In a saucepan, bring shortening, butter, water, and cocoa to boil. Pour over the flour mixture while still hot. Add beaten eggs, buttermilk, soda, cinnamon, and vanilla. Bake in 9 x 13 glass casserole dish at 350 degrees for 30 to 35 minutes. While cake is baking make frosting:

1 stick butter (or oleo)
1 or 2 tablespoons cocoa
6 tablespoons Pet milk
1 box powdered sugar
1 teaspoon vanilla
1 cup chopped walnuts

Bring oleo, cocoa, and milk to a boil. Add powdered sugar, vanilla, and nuts. Spread over cake while both are hot.

Taught to me by my sister-in-law Marie Meier.

CHOCOLATE CAKE

2 cups flour
1 cup water
1/4 cup shortening
4 oz. melted chocolate
1 1/4 teaspoons baking soda
2 cups sugar
3/4 cup sour cream
2 eggs
1 teaspoon vanilla
1 teaspoon baking powder

Preheat oven to 350 degrees. Lightly grease two 8-inch round cake pans. In large bowl combine all dry ingredients mixing well. Add chocolate, water, beaten eggs, shortening, and vanilla. Beat for 2 minutes at high speed, stirring well. Pour into cake pans and bake for 40-45 minutes. Cool cake completely. Slice layers with string. Frost with your favorite frosting.

Taught to me by my mother Mildred Lee.

ANGEL FOOD CAKE

1 cup cake flour
1 1/2 cups egg whites
2 1/2 tablespoons cold water
1 1/2 teaspoons cream of tartar
1 1/2 cups sugar
1/2 teaspoon salt
1 teaspoon vanilla

Sift flour and 1/2 cup sugar together. Place egg whites in a large bowl and add salt and water. Whip until stiff peaks form. Add cream of tartar, whip until mixture stands in peaks. Whip in remaining sugar. Fold in part of the flour mixture. Add vanilla and remaining flour mixture. Pour batter into ungreased angel food cake pan. Bake 40 to 50 minutes at 350 degrees. Invert cake pan until cake is cool.

Taught to me by my mother Mildred Lee.

ONE BOWL SCRATCH CAKE

1/2 cup shortening
1 teaspoon baking powder
1 1/2 cups sugar
2 eggs
2 1/4 cups self-rising flour (sifted)
1/4 teaspoon salt
1 cup milk
1 1/4 teaspoons vanilla

Stir shortening just enough to soften. Sift in dry ingredients. Add about 3/4 cup milk and mix with mixer until flour is dampened. Beat 2 minutes. Add unbeaten eggs and remaining milk, beat 1 minute longer and add vanilla. Pour batter in greased floured pans and bake at 375 degrees about 25 minutes (for layers about 35 minutes). This cake can be used with many different frostings.

Taught to me by Hazel Hall.

MISSISSIPPI MUD CAKE

2 sticks butter, melted
4 eggs, slightly beaten
1 1/2 cups plain flour
1 1/2 cups pecans, chopped
1/2 cup cocoa
2 cups sugar
1 teaspoon vanilla
1/2 teaspoon salt

Mix together sugar, cocoa, and butter and add eggs. Add flour, pecans, vanilla, and salt to above. Bake 35 minutes at 350 degrees in a greased 9 x 13 oblong pan.

TOPPING

Cover with miniature marshmallows and return to oven to melt marshmallows.

Cream:

1/2 cup milk
1/3 cup cocoa
1 stick melted butter
1 box powdered sugar

Sift cocoa and powdered sugar, add milk and butter. Mix until smooth, then put on top of cake.

Taught to me by my mother Mildred Lee.

SOFT MOLASSES CAKE

2 1/2 cups sifted all-purpose flour
1 3/4 teaspoons baking soda
1/2 teaspoon ground ginger
1/2 teaspoon ground cinnamon
1/2 cup shortening
1 cup boiling water
1/8 teaspoon ground cloves
1/4 teaspoon salt
1 cup sugar
1 cup molasses
2 eggs, well beaten

Sift flour, salt, spices, and soda and set aside. Cream sugar with shortening and molasses until well blended. Add dry ingredients to creamed mixture alternately with boiling water. Stir in eggs. Pour into a well greased 13 x 9 x 2-inch baking pan and bake at 350 degrees for 30 minutes. Frost with canned or dried apples.

Taught to me by my great-grandmother, Malinda Allens. Growing up, my great-grandmother lived with my grand-parents, my mother, Carolyn, and I. I thought Carolyn and I were good kids but Grandma Lindy said otherwise. The preacher came to eat on Sundays and it never failed that Grandma Lindy told him every time he came just how mean and hard to control Carolyn and I were. Do you believe that??

JAM CAKE

1/2 cup butter
1 cup buttermilk
3 eggs
1 teaspoon vanilla
1/2 teaspoon salt
2 cups sugar
3 cups cake flour
1 1/4 teaspoons soda
1/2 teaspoon nutmeg
2 cups jam (your favorite)

Cream butter, sugar, and salt. Sift and add flour, soda, nutmeg, and eggs. While beating, gradually add buttermilk and vanilla, then the jam. Pour in well greased tube or bundt pan. Bake 300 degrees for 45-50 minutes (no longer). While cake is still hot, glaze with the following:

1/4 lb. butter
1 cup sugar
1/3 cup milk
1/4 teaspoon salt

Bring these ingredients to a hard boil. Pour half on the cake while hot. Cool the other half until it forms a soft ball. Pour on cake to glaze.

Taught to me by my mother Mildred Lee.

MOLASSES APPLE STACK CAKE

2 1/2 cups flour
2 teaspoons baking powder
1/2 cup shortening
3/4 cup molasses
1 cup sugar
1/2 teaspoon each salt and soda
2 eggs
Spice (ginger or whatever you prefer)

Cream shortening and sugar. Add eggs and molasses. Stir together flour, baking powder, salt, soda, and spices. Add to creamed mixture and mix well. Pour onto floured cloth. Knead until dough is stiff. Roll out five small balls. Place in five greased and floured 9-inch cake pans (layers will be thin). Bake at 350 degrees for 10 to 12 minutes. Cook dried apples and spices to taste. Stack cake with apples between layers.

Taught to me by my step-grandmother, Auda Lee. When I was very small we sharecropped some land from Peepaw's father where we raised cotton. Auda was a great cook with what little she had to work with. My mother would always tell me when we went over there to stay out of her way and to not ask for anything to eat. Auda would set me on a home-made table carved out of wood by hand and let me watch her make this cake. I can close my eyes and almost taste it still today.

CAKE FROM SCRATCH

2 cups self-rising flour
1/2 cup shortening
1 1/2 teaspoons vanilla
1 1/2 cups sugar
7/8 cup sweet milk
2 eggs

Sift flour and sugar together twice. Add shortening and blend. Add 2/3 cup milk, and beat well. Add eggs and remaining milk and beat well. Grease and flour 2 cake pans. Bake at 350 degrees until toothpick comes out clean. Top with favorite icing.

Taught to me by my mother Mildred Lee.

FAVORITE COCONUT CAKE

3 cups sifted cake flour
2 cups sugar
1 cup milk
1/4 teaspoon salt
1 cup butter
4 eggs
1 teaspoon vanilla
4 teaspoons baking powder

Sift flour three times with baking powder and salt. Cream butter thoroughly. Add sugar gradually, cream well, and add vanilla. Add eggs one at a time beating after each egg. Add dry ingredients, alternating with milk. Pour into two greased and floured round cake pans. Bake at 375 degrees for 25 minutes. Frost with your favorite icing or bake in a baking dish and frost with 1 layer coconut cream and 1 can of Eagle Brand milk. Top with Cool Whip, then a layer of frozen coconut.

Taught to me by my mother Mildred Lee.

GRANNY'S BEST WHITE SCRATCH CAKE

6 egg whites
2 1/2 teaspoons baking powder*
1/2 cup shortening (1/2 butter,
   1/2 Crisco)
1/2 teaspoon butter flavoring
2 1/2 cups cake flour
1 teaspoon salt*
1 teaspoon vanilla
1 teaspoon almond extract

Heat oven to 350 degrees. Grease and flour cake pans or sheet cake pan. Beat egg whites in a large bowl until stiff. Beat remaining ingredients, except milk, in another large bowl on medium speed, scraping bowl occasionally for two minutes. Fold batter into egg whites. Pour into pan and bake 30-35 minutes. Cool completely and frost with chocolate whipped frosting or decorator frosting for the holidays.

*If using self-rising flour, omit baking powder and salt.

CARROT CAKE

1 1/2 cups salad oil
4 eggs
2 teaspoons baking powder
1 teaspoon salt
1 cup pecans
2 cups granulated sugar
2 cups flour
2 teaspoons cinnamon
3 cups grated carrots

Combine oil and sugar together. Add eggs one at a time, beating after each. Sift together flour and other dry ingredients. Fold in carrots and nuts. Grease and flour three 9-inch cake pans. Bake at 350 degrees for 40 minutes.

ICING

1 6-oz. package cream cheese
1 6-oz. confectioners sugar
1/2 stick margarine

Blend all ingredients together, then spread over cake.

Taught to me by my mother Mildred Lee.

COLA CAKE

2 cups flour
1 cup (2 sticks) margarine
1 cup cola
2 beaten eggs
1 teaspoon soda
Pinch salt
2 cups sugar
2 tablespoons cocoa powder
1/2 cup buttermilk
1 teaspoon vanilla
1 1/2 cups miniature marshmallows

Combine flour and sugar. Heat margarine, cocoa powder, and cola until mixture boils. Pour mixture over flour and sugar. Blend and add buttermilk, eggs, soda, and vanilla. Fold in marshmallows. Beat well by hand and pour into 13 x 9-inch baking pan. Bake 30-40 minutes at 350 degrees. Frost while hot.

COLA ICING

1/2 cup (1 stick) margarine
6 tablespoons cola
Nuts (if desired)
3 tablespoons cocoa powder
1 box (1 lb.) powdered sugar

Combine margarine, cocoa powder, and cola. Bring to boil in small pan. Pour powdered sugar and mix well. Fold in nuts. Spread on hot cake.

EXTRA MOIST PINEAPPLE
UPSIDE-DOWN CAKE

1 can (20 oz.) sliced pineapple
   in juice
2 pkgs. (4 serving size) vanilla flavor
   instant pudding and pie filling
10 maraschino cherry halves
1/4 cup oil
1/2 cup firmly-packed brown sugar
1 pkg. yellow cake mix
4 eggs
1 cup water

Drain pineapple, reserving juice. Arrange slices in 13 x 9-inch pan and place cherry half in center of each. Combine 1 pkg. pudding mix and pineapple juice, pour over pineapple, and sprinkle with brown sugar. Combine cake mix, remaining pudding mix, eggs, water, and oil in large mixer bowl. Blend, then beat at medium speed of electric mixer for 4 minutes. Pour into pan. Bake 350 degrees for 55 to 60 minutes or until cake tester inserted in center comes out clean and cake begins to pull away from sides of pan. (DO NOT OVERBAKE!) Cool in pan 5 minutes. Invert onto platter and let stand 1 minute, then remove pan. Serve warm.

BUTTERNUT POUND CAKE

1 cup shortening
2 1/2 cups plain flour
1 cup sweet milk
4 eggs
2 cups sugar
1/2 cup self-rising flour
1 tablespoon butternut flavoring

Cream shortening, sugar, and eggs for 1 or 2 minutes on high speed. Add flour and milk alternately. Add flavoring. Bake in a 300-degree oven about 1 hour or until done. Cool and turn out of pan.

Gwen put this cake in the oven in a plastic dish one time and melted it all!

CHESS CAKE

1 box yellow cake mix
1 egg
1 stick margarine, melted

Mix together and press in an ungreased oblong cake pan. Mix 1 8-oz. package cream cheese, 2 eggs, 1 lb. powdered sugar. Mix together, pour over cake mixture, and bake at 350 degrees 35 to 38 minutes or until knife comes out clean.

Taught to me by my sister-in-law Vi Whitlatch.

REFRIGERATOR CAKE

2 egg yolks, beaten (slightly)
2 cups sugar
1 cup chopped pecans
1 medium can crushed pineapple
 (drained)
1 cup butter
1 teaspoon vanilla
1 lb. vanilla wafers

Cream butter and sugar until fluffy. Add egg yolks and beat until light. Add pineapple, pecans, and vanilla. Crumble wafers fine and place ingredients in a large glass bowl or baking dish. Lay a layer of wafers and layer of cake mixture. Keep refrigerated until served. Serve with Cool Whip and top with maraschino cherries, if desired.

Taught to me by my mother-in-law Arah Richardson.

BETTER-THAN-SEX CAKE

Bake 1 yellow cake mix. Take 1 large can crushed pineapple and 1 cup sugar, cook until thick. Put on cake. Fix 1 large box vanilla instant pudding and spread on cake, top with 1 large Cool Whip. Sprinkle with nuts and coconut. Garnish with maraschino cherries.

Taught to me by my sister-in-law Vi Whitlach.

OLD FASHIONED
UPSIDE-DOWN CAKE

2/3 cup butter
2/3 cup packed brown sugar
1 can (20 oz.) Dole sliced pineapple
   in syrup
10 maraschino cherries
2 eggs, separated
3/4 cup granulated sugar
1 teaspoon fresh grated lemon peel
1 teaspoon fresh lemon juice
1 teaspoon vanilla extract
1 1/2 cups flour
1 3/4 teaspoons baking powder
1/4 teaspoon salt
1/2 cup dairy sour cream

Melt 1/3 cup butter in 10-inch cast iron skillet. Remove from heat. Add brown sugar and stir until well blended. Drain pineapple well, reserving 2 tablespoons syrup. Arrange pineapple slices in butter-sugar mixture. Place cherry in center. Beat egg whites to soft peaks. Gradually beat in 1/4 cup granulated sugar to make stiff meringue. With same beater, beat remaining 1/3 cup butter with remaining 1/2 cup sugar until fluffy. Beat in egg yolks, lemon peel and juice, and vanilla. Combine flour, baking powder, and salt. Blend into creamed mixture alternately with sour cream and 2 tablespoons pineapple syrup. Fold in egg white mixture. Pour over pineapple in skillet. Bake in 350-degree oven about 35 minutes until cake tests done. Let stand 10 minutes. Invert onto serving plate. Allow syrup to drain before removing skillet. Serve warm or cold.

Makes 8 servings.

MAHOGANY CAKE

Mix:

1/2 cup cocoa
1/2 cup canned milk
1/2 cup sugar
1 egg yolk

Stir well, then cook, stirring until thick. Cool.

Cream:

1 cup butter
1/4 teaspoon salt
1 cup sugar
2 egg yolks

Add 1 teaspoon soda in 1 cup buttermilk and add to creamed mixture. Add 2 cups flour, stir well, then add to first part of cooked mixture. Bake in 2 greased 9-inch cake pans at 350 degrees for approximately 30 minutes. Frost with your own favorite frosting.

Taught to me by my mother-in-law Arah Richardson.

PISTACHIO CAKE

Mix together:

1 box yellow cake mix
1 cup club soda
1/2 cup nuts
3 eggs
1 cup cooking oil

Bake at 350 degrees for approximately 45 minutes (in bundt pan). Let cool 15 minutes and remove from pan. Cut into 3 layers and ice in between, then on top and all over. Stuff hole in middle with leftover frosting.

FROSTING

1 large carton of Cool Whip
1 large pistachio instant pudding mix
1 1/2 cups cold milk

Whip pistachio pudding mix with milk. Stir in Cool Whip and frost cake. For Christmas, garnish with maraschino cherries.

Taught to me by Jan Corrigan.

SAUERKRAUT SURPRISE CAKE

2/3 cup butter or margarine
1 1/2 cups sugar
3 eggs
1/2 cup cocoa
1 cup water
1 8-oz. can (1 cup) sauerkraut
   (drained), rinsed and finely-snipped
1/4 teaspoon salt
1 teaspoon soda
1 teaspoon baking powder
1 teaspoon vanilla
2 cups flour

In large bowl, cream butter and sugar. Beat in eggs one at a time and add vanilla. Sift flour, soda, baking powder, salt, and cocoa. Add to creamed mixture alternately with water, beating after each addition. Stir in sauerkraut. Turn into greased 13 x 9 x 2 baking dish. Bake on 350 degrees for 35 to 40 minutes. Cool in pan.

Frost with sour cream chocolate frosting. Cut in squares to serve. The sauerkraut adds moistness and coconut-like texture.

Taught to me by my sister-in-law Vi Whitlach.

ECLAIR CAKE

1 box graham crackers
3 1/2 cups milk
2 packages or 1 large French vanilla
pudding (instant)
1 9-oz. carton Cool Whip

Butter 9 x 13 pan and line with graham crackers. Mix pudding with milk and beat on medium speed 2 minutes. Blend in Cool Whip. Pour half of the mixture over crackers and place second layer of crackers over pudding. Pour remaining pudding over crackers and cover with more crackers.

TOPPING

2 packages Redi Blend unsweetened
chocolate (in bags)
3 tablespoons softened margarine
3 teaspoons milk
2 teaspoons white syrup
2 teaspoons vanilla
1 1/2 cups powdered sugar

Mix real well. Put on cake and refrigerate 24 hours.

Taught to me by my sister-in-law Vi Whitlach.

QUICK MIX CAKE

Sift together:

2 cups sifted flour
1 cup sugar
2 teaspoons baking powder
1 teaspoon salt
1 teaspoon cinnamon
1/2 teaspoon nutmeg

Blend in 1/2 cup shortening

Break two whole eggs into a small bowl. To the eggs add one generous cup of crushed bananas, 1/4 teaspoon soda, and 1 teaspoon vanilla extract. Beat eggs, fruit, soda, and extract until light. Stir the egg mixture into the dry ingredients just enough to moisten. (Do not beat; this batter is supposed to be lumpy.) Pour batter into a cake pan, place on middle rack of 350-degree oven for 20 to 30 minutes.

You may judge when the cake is done by pressing on the top gently with your finger. If it springs back, it is done. When cool, ice with Angel Icing.

ANGEL ICING

1 cup white corn syrup
2 egg whites
1/4 teaspoon tartar
1 teaspoon vanilla

Heat corn syrup in saucepan until it comes to a rolling boil. With electric mixer on high speed, or with rotary beater, beat egg whites until they form stiff peaks. Add the cream of tartar foam when it first becomes frosty. Slowly add syrup while continuing to beat until icing forms stiff peaks. Fold in vanilla. The longer this icing is beaten, the stiffer it becomes.

MANDARIN ORANGE CAKE

1 Duncan Hines butter yellow cake mix
3/4 cup oil or margarine
3 eggs
1 can of mandarin oranges (juice and all)

ICING

1 large can crushed pineapple (drained)
1 9-oz. carton Cool Whip
1 large box of French vanilla instant pudding mix

Mix cake mix, eggs, oil, and mandarin oranges together. Bake in 3 layers at 350 degrees for 30 minutes. To prepare icing, drain pineapple and add instant pudding (dry). Fold in Cool Whip and put on cake. Keep refrigerated.

Taught to me by my sister-in-law Vi Whitlatch.

DEVILS FOOD CAKE

1 1/2 cups flour
1/2 cup cocoa
1/4 teaspoon cream of tartar
2/3 cup shortening
1 teaspoon vanilla
1 1/4 cups sugar
1 1/4 teaspoons soda
1 teaspoon salt
1 cup milk
2 eggs

Mix together dry ingredients in mixing bowl. Add shortening and 3/4 cup milk, vanilla, and eggs. Beat on medium speed about 2 minutes. Add 1/4 cup milk and beat two more minutes. Pour into 2 round cake pans that have been greased and floured. Bake at 350 degrees for about 25 minutes. Frost with white frosting, chocolate, caramel, or may be put together with whipped cream or Cool Whip. Refrigerate.

Taught to me by my mother Mildred Lee.

PINTO BEAN CAKE

1 cup sugar
1 stick oleo
1 egg
2 cups pinto beans, cooked
   and mashed
1 cup flour
1 teaspoon soda
1/2 teaspoon salt
1 teaspoon cinnamon
1/2 teaspoon cloves
2 cups raw apples, peeled and diced
1 cup raisins
1/2 cup nuts
1 teaspoon vanilla

Cream sugar and oleo. Add egg and beans. Sift dry ingredients together. Add to cream mixture along with apples, raisins, nuts, and vanilla. Bake for 1 hour.

FROSTING

1 box powdered sugar
1/2 cup oleo
1 tablespoon bean juice
1 teaspoon vanilla

Combine and spread on cake.

PRUNE CAKE

3 eggs
1 cup Wesson oil
1 1/2 cups sugar
1 cup cooked prunes, seeded
  and chopped
1 cup chopped nuts
2 cups flour
1 teaspoon salt
1 teaspoon cinnamon
1 teaspoon nutmeg
1 teaspoon allspice
1 teaspoon vanilla
1 teaspoon soda, mixed in 1 cup
  of buttermilk

Cream Wesson oil and sugar, and add eggs which have been beaten. Sift all of the dry ingredients together and add alternately with buttermilk and prunes. Beat well. Bake in two layers for 40 minutes in a 300-degree oven.

FROSTING FOR PRUNE CAKE

1 cup sugar
1/2 cup buttermilk
1/2 teaspoon soda
1 stick oleo
1 tablespoon Karo syrup
1 teaspoon vanilla

Mix all ingredients and cook in double boiler until it forms a soft ball in cool water.

JELL-O CAKE

1 box cake mix (yellow or white)
3/4 cup Wesson oil
4 eggs
1 small box Jell-o (any flavor)
3/4 cup milk

Bake at 350 degrees for 45 minutes in tube pan.

Taught to me by Sandra & Gerald Jetton.

BUTTERMILK CARAMEL ICING

2 cups sugar
1 cup buttermilk into which
  1 teaspoon of soda has
  been dissolved
1 cup butter
1 teaspoon vanilla flavoring

Combine sugar, milk, and butter and cook until soft ball stage. Add vanilla. Cool and beat until thick and creamy. Spread rapidly.

Taught to me by my mother Mildred Lee.

BRENDA'S CARAMEL ICING

3 cups sugar
1 teaspoon vanilla flavoring
1 1/2 cups milk
1/2 stick margarine

In skillet (preferably iron) melt 1/2 cup of sugar. Mix the remaining 2 1/2 cups sugar and milk. When sugar is melted, add more milk to mixture. Cook until soft ball forms in water. Remove from heat, add margarine and vanilla. Stir until cooled and slightly hardened. Delicious icing with yellow cake.

Taught to me by Brenda Hall.

7 MINUTE ICING

3/4 cup sugar
1/3 cup white Karo syrup
1 cup small marshmallows
2 tablespoons water
1/4 teaspoon salt
1 teaspoon vanilla
2 egg whites
1/4 teaspoon cream of tartar

Mix all ingredients in top of double boiler. Beat with electric mixer for 7 minutes. Recipe may be doubled.

COOKED ICING

2 egg whites
3/4 cup sugar
1/3 cup corn syrup
2 tablespoons water
1/4 teaspoon salt
1/4 teaspoon cream of tartar

Put all the above ingredients in a double boiler. While cooking, beat until it stands in peaks (approximately 5 minutes). Remove from heat, add 1 teaspoon vanilla, and continue beating until thick enough to spread.

CHOCOLATE ICING
OR HOT FUDGE SUNDAE SAUCE

2 cups sugar
1/2 cup Crisco
Dash of salt
2 tablespoons cocoa
2/3 cup milk

Combine dry ingredients and mix well. Add liquids. Bring to a fast boil and cook 1 1/2 minutes. Remove from heat, set pan in cool water (in sink), and beat until desired consistency. Serve warm as sauce or cool completely and beat until ready to put on cool cake.

Taught to me by Gerald and Sandra Jetton.

QUICK CHOCOLATE ICING

1/4 cup milk
1/4 cup cocoa
1/4 stick oleo
1 cup sugar

Mix all ingredients in heavy saucepan. Boil 1 minute and remove from heat. Beat until spreading consistency, adding 1 teaspoon vanilla while beating. (Excellent on sheet cake.)

Taught to me by my mother Mildred Lee.

PARTY CAKE ICING

1/3 cup water
1 1/2 lbs. confectioners sugar
1 cup Crisco
1/4 teaspoon vanilla extract

Beat ingredients until smooth. Add desired food coloring to any amount of the mixture for decorating. Double amount if for a large cake.

Taught to me by my mother Mildred Lee.

BANANA PUDDING

1 12 oz. box vanilla wafers
2 1/2 cups sugar
6 cups milk
6 bananas, sliced
1 cup self-rising flour
6 eggs, separated
1 teaspoon vanilla

Crumble enough vanilla wafers to cover the bottom of 9 x 13-inch glass baking dish to 1-inch thickness. Set aside.

Preheat oven to 350 degrees.

Combine flour and 2 cups sugar in top of a double boiler and mix thoroughly. Add egg yolks and mix well. Gradually add milk to the mixture and blend until smooth. Add vanilla and cook over simmering water at medium temperature until thickened, stirring continuously. Allow to cool to room temperature. Pour mixture over wafers and cover evenly with sliced bananas.

Beat egg whites in mixing bowl, gradually adding remaining 1/2 cup sugar. Beat until stiff. Spread meringue over bananas and brown for 8 to 10 minutes.

Makes 8 servings.

In the year 1977 I was dating Burt Reynolds (I hope he doesn't mind my telling this), and he came to my home for dinner. I thought I was really showing off my cooking talents and I cooked a banana pudding, not knowing his condition of low blood sugar (hypoglycemia). He passed out on me due to the pudding and so much sugar. Well, at least I can say it was a very different date!

Around Nashville I'm known best for this dish.

PINEAPPLE, BANANA PUDDING

1 12-oz. box of vanilla wafers
3/4 cup self-rising flour
2 1/2 cups sugar
6 eggs, separated
6 cups milk
1 teaspoon vanilla
6 bananas, sliced
1 16-oz. can of chunky pineapple,
  drained

Crumble enough vanilla wafers to cover bottom of 9 x 13-inch glass baking dish to 1 inch thickness. Set aside. Preheat oven to 350 degrees.

Combine flour and 2 cups sugar in top of a double boiler and mix thoroughly. Add egg yolks and mix well. Gradually add milk to the mixture and blend until smooth. Add vanilla and cook over simmering water at medium temperature until thickened, stirring continuously. Allow to cool to room temperature. Pour mixture over wafers and cover evenly with bananas and drained can of chunky pineapple.

Beat egg whites in mixing bowl gradually adding remaining 1/2 cup of sugar. Beat until stiff. Spread meringue over bananas and pineapple and brown in oven for 5 minutes or so.

Serves 8.

OLD FASHIONED
BISCUIT PUDDING

**3 large biscuits, crumbled
  (already baked)
1 cup sugar
1 teaspoon vanilla
2 cups milk
4 eggs, well beaten
1/4 cup melted oleo or butter**

Combine all ingredients and mix well. Pour into 1 1/2 quart casserole dish. Pour 1/2 inch water in baking pan and place casserole in pan. Bake at 350 degrees for 1 hour.

Taught to me by my mother Mildred Lee.

PINEAPPLE PUDDING

Use recipe for banana pudding for your filling. Instead of using bananas use 2 small cans of crushed pineapple (drained). For topping, beat six egg whites, add 1/2 cup of sugar, place on top of filling, and brown.

Use ovenproof dish. Crumble 1 package of vanilla wafers on bottom of dish and pour filling on top. Pour egg whites on top and brown.

RICE PUDDING

1 1/2 cups cooked rice
   (not minute rice)
3/4 cup raisins
1/2 cup sugar
2 eggs, beaten
1/4 teaspoon vanilla
2 cups milk, scalded
2 tablespoons melted butter

Mix first 5 ingredients. Add scalded milk and butter. (You may add a dash of cinnamon and nutmeg.) Pour into 1 1/2 quart casserole dish. Bake at 350 degrees for about 1 hour or until mixture is firm. Makes 6 servings.

Taught to me by my mother Mildred Lee.

PISTACHIO PUDDING OR SALAD
(OR WATERGATE SALAD)

1 large package pistachio
   instant pudding mix
add 1 large Cool Whip
2 cups of colored miniature
   marshmallows
1 20-oz. can crushed pineapple
   (mix with dry pudding mix)
1 cup nuts

Mix well and refrigerate.

Taught to me by my sister-in-law Vi Whitlatch. She made this very often for my girls. They loved it!!

KAPNER'S COCONUT PUDDING

1 1/2 cups grated coconut
3 egg yolks
1/4 cup sugar
1 cup condensed milk
1 teaspoon vanilla
1 cup bread crumbs
3 egg whites
1 tablespoon butter
1 cup water

Use fresh coconut. Let the milk out of the coconut by punching holes into two of the eyes and draining. Then place entire coconut in 200-degree oven for 10 minutes. This loosens the meat inside the shell enough so that when you break it open, much of the meat is already loose. It can then be easily grated by hand or in a food processor. If you like the pudding a little thicker, add more bread crumbs.

Mix the sugar and egg yolks. Add butter. Add condensed milk and water. Add bread crumbs, coconut, and vanilla. Pour into buttered ovenproof baking dish and bake at 300 degrees for 30 minutes. Beat the egg whites with 2 tablespoons of sugar and a pinch of cream of tartar until stiff. Spread over the pudding and brown in a preheated 350-degree oven for 5 to 10 minutes.

GERMAN CHOCOLATE PUDDING
A-la-Mee Maw
(My children could eat this every day)

1 4 oz. bar German Sweet Chocolate
1/4 lb. butter
3 eggs, separated
1 10-oz. box vanilla wafers
1 cup powdered sugar
1 pint whipping cream
1 teaspoon vanilla

Melt butter and chocolate together. Add chocolate mixture to beaten egg yolks. Add 2/3 cup powdered sugar, mix well, and chill. Whip cream and fold into mixture. Beat egg whites until standing in peaks. Add 1/3 cup remaining sugar to egg whites and fold into chocolate mixture. Grind or crush vanilla wafers. Line one 9 x 9-inch-deep dish with part of wafer crumbs. Spread 2 cups of chocolate mixture over wafers. Add another layer of crumbs and repeat until all mixture is used, topping with crumbs. Refrigerate 24 hours before serving.

Gwen, my oldest daughter, thinks this can be fixed on the spur of a moment but it takes 24 hours. Instead of a hug and a hello from her, I get, "Where's the pudding, mom?"

GRATED SWEET POTATO
PUDDING

4 cups grated sweet potatoes
1 cup butter, melted
1 teaspoon vanilla
2 cups sugar
1 cup pecans
4 eggs, well-beaten
1/4 teaspoon nutmeg
1/4 teaspoon salt
2 cups milk

Add sugar to grated sweet potatoes. Then combine eggs, milk, and butter. Pour over sweet potato mixture and mix well. Add vanilla, pecans, nutmeg, and salt and mix again. Pour into greased 13 x 9 x 2-inch baking dish and cook for 2 hours at 300 degrees.

Taught to me by my mother, Mildred Lee. This pudding tastes totally different from other sweet potato dishes. I don't know anyone except members of my family that cooks this dish.

EGG CUSTARD

4 eggs
2 tablespoons flour
1 teaspoon vanilla
1 cup sugar
1 cup milk
nutmeg on top (optional)

Beat eggs until foamy, then add sugar, flour, and milk. Add vanilla, beat again and pour into pie shell, unbaked. Bake 45 minutes at 350 degrees.

Taught to me by my mother Mildred Lee.

OLD-FASHIONED EGG CUSTARD

1 cup sugar
2 tablespoons flour
1/2 teaspoon salt
3/4 teaspoon nutmeg
3 eggs
2 cups sweet milk
3/4 stick margarine or butter
    (melted)

Mix all dry ingredients. Add eggs and milk; mix well. Add melted butter and mix again. Pour into unbaked pie shell. Bake 45 minutes at 350 degrees, then lower temperature to 200 degrees for 15 more minutes.

APPLE SAUCE JELL-O SALAD

1 can apple sauce (#303 can)
2 cups 7-Up
1/3 cup red hots
2 packages lemon Jell-o

Heat 7-Up with red hots until dissolved. Pour over Jell-o, mix well and let cool. Add apple sauce and refrigerate until firm. (Can also use strawberry Jell-o.)

This is a very good light dessert for a hot summer day – serve with fancy cookies.

Taught to me by my sister-in-law Vi Whitlatch.

PUMPKIN TART

12 graham crackers (crushed – 1 cup)
1/2 cup margarine
1/3 cup sugar

Press above into 9 x 13 ungreased pan. Preheat oven to 350 degrees.

1st layer:

2 eggs
8 oz. Philadelphia cream cheese
    (room temperature)
3/4 cup sugar

Mix and pour over crust. Bake 20 minutes and cool.

Middle layer:

2 cups pumpkin
1/2 cup sugar
1/2 teaspoon salt
1/4 teaspoon nutmeg
3 egg yolks (reserve whites)
1/2 cup milk
2 teaspoons cinnamon

Mix in saucepan at medium heat. Cook until thick. Add 1 envelope plain gelatin, dissolved in 1/4 cup cold water and cook.

Beat 3 reserved whites with 1/4 cup sugar until stiff. Fold mixture into pumpkin mixture. Then pour above ingredients over crust and cream cheese mixture. Top with whipped cream or Cool Whip. Refrigerate 12 hours before serving.

Taught to me by my niece Brenda Kennedy.

WALNUT BOURBON BALLS

1 stick butter
Walnuts, chopped well
1 box powdered sugar
Bourbon to mix

Sift powdered sugar. Mix powdered sugar and butter and add bourbon. (If you used too much bourbon add more powdered sugar.) Roll into balls in walnuts.

GREAT FOR PARTIES AND HOLIDAYS!

Taught to me by my sister-in-law Marie Meier.

COCONUT BALLS

1 stick butter
1 cup crushed nuts
1/2 teaspoon vanilla
1 carton Cool Whip
1 cup sugar
1 large can crushed pineapple
1 can coconut
Vanilla wafers

Melt butter in pan. Add nuts, drained pineapple, and sugar. Stir over medium heat until sugar is dissolved. Chill.

Use 3 vanilla wafers per ball. Spread filling between each cookie. Ice with Cool Whip and sprinkle with coconut.

Taught to me by my friend Maxine Hyder.

FOUR LAYER DESSERT

1st Layer:

1 stick butter
1/2 cup pecans
1 tablespoon self-rising flour

Mix and bake 15 minutes at 350 degrees in 8-inch oblong pan.

2nd Layer:

1 8-oz. package cream cheese
   (room temperature)
1 cup confectioners sugar

Mix with mixer and add small carton of Cool Whip (4 1/2 oz.).

3rd Layer:

1 large package instant chocolate
   pudding (3 oz.). Use instructions
   on box.

4th Layer:

1 large carton Cool Whip

Garnish with pecans. Put in large pyrex dish.

Taught to me by my mother Mildred Lee.

BASIC BROWNIES
(soft & chewy)

2/3 cup sifted all-purpose flour
1/4 teaspoon salt
2 squares Bakers Unsweetened
   Chocolate or 4 tablespoons cocoa
1 teaspoon vanilla
1/2-1 cup chocolate chips
1/2 teaspoon baking powder
1/3 cup butter or Crisco
1 cup sugar
2 eggs, well beaten
1/2 cup broken walnuts or pecans

Mix dry ingredients together and set aside. Melt shortening and chocolate over hot water. Beat sugar and eggs together, add chocolate mixture, then flour mixture. Stir in nuts, chocolate chips and vanilla. Pour in greased pan and bake for 25 minutes at 350 degrees. (Will not cook firm like cake; will be waxy.) Cool and cut in squares. Can double this recipe using an 11 x 14 pan.

RICE CRISPIE SNACKS

1 package Rice Crispies cereal
2 sticks of butter
1 large package of big marshmallows
1 cup of crushed pecans (optional)

Melt butter and marshmallows in deep frying pan. Pour in box of Rice Crispies (add nuts if desired). Pour into buttered pan, let cool, and cut into squares.

CARAMEL POPCORN

6-8 quarts popped popcorn

CARAMEL

2 sticks oleo
1 teaspoon vanilla
1 teaspoon salt
1/2 cup white Karo syrup
2 cups brown sugar
1/2 teaspoon baking soda

Put all ingredients except vanilla and soda in saucepan. Bring to a boil, stirring constantly, until mixture reaches the boiling stage. After it comes to a boil, let cook 5 minutes without stirring. Stir in soda and vanilla then pour over popped corn in a very large container. Stir carefully and bake for 1 hour in 250-degree oven. Stir every 15 minutes. Remove from oven and break corn apart. Let cool. Place in plastic bags or jars with tight-fitting lids.

EDIBLE PLAY DOUGH

2 cups of peanut butter
2 1/2 cups of powdered milk
2 cups of white Karo syrup
2 1/2 cups of powdered sugar

Mix well.

GREAT FOR KIDS . . . 1 to 90!

PEANUT BUTTER COOKIES

1/4 cup shortening
1 cup peanut butter
1/2 cup brown sugar (packed)
3/4 teaspoon soda
1/4 teaspoon salt
1/4 cup butter or margarine
1/2 cup granulated sugar
1 1/4 cup plain flour
1/2 teaspoon baking powder

Mix thoroughly shortening, butter, granulated sugar, brown sugar, peanut butter, and egg. Blend in flour, soda, baking powder, and salt. Cover and chill. Heat oven to 375 degrees. Shape dough into 1″ balls. Place on lightly greased baking sheet. With a fork dipped in flour, flatten in criss-cross pattern. Bake 10 to 12 minutes. This recipe can be doubled and 1/2 of it frozen. (If using self-rising flour omit soda, salt and baking powder.)

This was given to me by Luoma Kent, a wonderful friend of the family. She used to cook in the lunchroom where I went to high school. I would go back and ask for seconds and thirds. She is still a wonderful cook, along with her husband. Her children and I used to play together as kids.

GINGER SNAPS

3/4 cup shortening
1 egg
2 cups sifted self-rising flour
1 teaspoon cinnamon
1 cup sugar
1/4 cup homemade molasses
1 1/2 teaspoons soda
1 teaspoon ginger

Cream shortening, add sugar gradually, and cream thoroughly. Add unbeaten eggs and molasses and mix until smooth. Sift flour, soda, and spices into creamed mixture and mix well with hands. Roll out on floured dough board until fairly thin and cut. Bake 350 degrees on ungreased pan until light brown.

These cookies are delicious and crisp. Watch them carefully; they get overdone in a hurry.

Dough will be real soft when it is put on dough board. Knead it a little so you can handle it better.

Taught to me by Hazel Hall.

CHOCOLATE ROLLS

1 1/2 cups Crisco
pinch of salt
2 cups water

Flour stirred into the desired consistency so you can knead it good. Divide dough into 1/3. Roll out and spread with following:

1 stick margarine, melted
(this is enough for all 3 rolls)

Sprinkle with 1 cup sugar and 1/4 cup cocoa to each roll. Roll up, pinch ends together, and prick with a fork. Bake at 300 degrees for 30 minutes. Turn oven to 375 degrees for another 30 minutes.

Taught to me by my mother-in-law, Arah Richardson. When Richey and I married he told me about his mother's chocolate rolls and divinity peanut butter rolls. I soon found out how wonderful they really were. A few years ago we went to Mom's for Christmas and Richey's sister, Vi, made both chocolate rolls and peanut butter divinity. Soon after they were finished they came up missing! Richey hid them in secret places all over the house where only he knew they were. The whole family looked all day for them while he would slip out and get pieces and taunt us with them. He had a ball and we had no dessert. This happens almost every time they are cooked. He wants all of them, not just part. He's never sure there's enough for anyone except himself.

PEANUT BUTTER FINGERS

1/2 cup butter
1/2 cup sugar
1/2 cup brown sugar
1 unbeaten egg
1/3 cup peanut butter
1/2 teaspoon soda
1/4 teaspoon salt
1/2 teaspoon vanilla
1 cup flour
1 cup rolled oats
1 cup (6-oz. package) semi-sweet
    chocolate bits
1/2 cup sifted confectioners sugar
1/4 cup peanut butter

Cream butter, adding both sugars. Add egg, 1/3 cup peanut butter, soda, salt, and vanilla. Add flour and rolled oats. Mix thoroughly.

Turn into 9 x 13″ pan, well greased and lightly floured on bottom. Bake 350 degrees for 25-30 minutes until lightly browned. Sprinkle immediately with chocolate pieces. Let stand 5 minutes. Spread evenly.

Combine confectioners sugar, 1/4 cup peanut butter, and milk. Mix well and drizzle peanut butter mixture over chocolate. Cool. Cut into 1 x 2 inch fingers. Makes 4 dozen.

APPLE ROLL

1/3 cup milk
1 1/2 cups butter flavored Crisco
1/2 teaspoon salt

Mix all ingredients and roll in circle. Sprinkle 2 cups chopped apples and 1 tablespoon cinnamon over dough and roll up like jelly roll. Cut in 1 1/2-inch pieces crimped on end and place in pan which has 1 stick of melted margarine. Bring 2 cups sugar and 2 cups of water to a rolling boil and pour over rolls. Bake at 350 degrees until brown.

DIVINITY PEANUT BUTTER ROLL

2 1/2 cups sugar
1/2 cup white syrup and
   1/2 cup water

Cook until forms hard ball in cold water. Have ready 3 egg whites beaten stiff. Pour 1/2 cup cooked syrup into egg whites and beat in well. Pour rest of syrup in. Add 1 teaspoon vanilla and continue beating. Have dough board covered with powdered sugar. When mixture is cool and thick enough to handle, pour onto powdered sugar, knead, and pat out to about 1/2 inch thick. Spread with peanut butter and roll like jelly roll. Let cool and slice.

Taught to me by my mother-in-law Arah Richardson.

FUDGE

4 cups sugar
3-4 tablespoons cocoa
4 tablespoons butter or oleo
1 large can milk
1/2 to 1 cup nuts
1 teaspoon vanilla

Mix sugar, cocoa, then add milk and butter. Cook slowly, stirring constantly until soft ball forms in cup of water. Cool and beat. Add vanilla and nuts. Turn out on buttered dish. When completely cooled, cut in squares.

Taught to me by Bonnie Wilson.

LAZY MAN'S COBBLER

3/4 stick margarine
1 cup self-rising flour
1 can of your favorite pie filling
1 cup milk
2 cups sugar

Mix all ingredients in large casserole dish and cook at 350 degrees until bubbly and the top browns. (I use a large can of sliced peaches.)

Taught to me by my mother Mildred Lee.

OLD FASHIONED COBBLER

**1 quart fresh sliced peaches,
   strawberries or blackberries
1 cup sugar
2 tablespoons oleo**

Put half the fruit in pan or corningware dish. Add 1 1/2 cups water, 1/2 cup sugar, and dot with 1 tablespoon oleo. Make up biscuit dough or you can use canned biscuits. (The dough is much better.) Roll out the dough and cover fruit with strips of dough. Repeat with the rest of the fruit, sugar, and oleo, but omit water. Make pie crust dough for top crust. Cover fruit with crust, rub top with a little oleo, and sprinkle a little sugar. Bake in a 350-degree oven until crust is brown.

Taught to me by my mother, Mildred Lee. When I was a kid my grandmother would send me to pick berries for pies, etc. One day I was pickin' – mad because I had to – and I wasn't paying any attention to what I was doing. I thrust my hand and arm into a big bunch of vines and withdrew my arm with a green garden snake wrapped around it. Needless to say, I threw the bucket of berries up in the air and Mama had to settle for either peach or apple.

WHOLE EGG COBBLER

2 1/2 cups milk
1 cup sugar
1/2 cup butter
1 teaspoon vanilla
1/4 teaspoon nutmeg
6 to 8 whole eggs

Mix first five ingredients in deep corningware dish. Heat to just under boiling point. Break eggs into the hot milk.

COBBLER DOUGH

2 cups self-rising flour. Blend in 2 sticks margarine. Add 3/4 cup buttermilk. Mix and divide into two parts. Roll 1 crust for top. Roll one half out thin, cut in strips, and add to mixture. Put top crust on. Make some slits in it for steam to escape. Rub crust with margarine and sprinkle with sugar. Cook in 325-degree oven until crust is golden brown.

> *Taught to me by Eva Basden. This dish goes back to my mother's childhood and was a favorite of my grandfather, Chester Russell. This was made when women had to use their imagination for something different. It's different and it's delicious!*

SWEET POTATO COBBLER

Peel and slice 4 medium-size red sweet potatoes. Place in deep medium-size saucepan, cover with water, and cook until tender. When potatoes are tender add 3 cups of sugar, reduce heat to medium, and continue to cook for about 10 minutes.

Using the recipe for pie dough, roll out dough very thin. Cut into 1-inch-pieces, 1/2 inch wide. Slowly drop each piece of dough into mixture and reduce heat to low. When all pieces of dough have thoroughly cooked, add 1 teaspoon of nutmeg and 1 teaspoon of cinnamon. Also add 1/2 stick of butter, stir, and remove from heat. Pour into an ovenproof deep dish. Cut strips of dough and place on top of mixture in desired pattern. When mixture is covered with dough strips, use squeeze butter and generously cover the strips of dough. Sprinkle 1/2 cup of sugar on top of dough, place in oven, and slowly brown dough. Cook on bake at 375 degrees until browned evenly. Cool or serve hot.

As a young girl we made cobblers out of just about everything. We raised our own sweet potatoes and to make sure we had them all winter, Daddy would dig a hole underneath the house and bury the potatoes, along with Irish (or white) potatoes, watermelons, and various dried food and cover them with lime. I hated having to go dig them out when company came.

SWEET POTATO PIE

1 deep dish pie crust
1 stick of butter
2 eggs
1 1/2 cups sugar
1 tablespoon vanilla
3 cups cooked sweet potatoes,
   mashed
1 small can of Carnation
   evaporated milk
1/4 teaspoon salt

Cut 4 medium-size sweet potatoes into quarters. Place in deep saucepan, cover with water, and cook until tender. Remove from pan and drain. Beat with electric mixer until smooth. Add butter, eggs, sugar, vanilla, and salt to potatoes. Beat with mixer until well blended. Gradually add evaporated milk and blend. Pour into deep dish uncooked pie shell. Bake at 350 degrees until brown and firm or until a toothpick inserted in the middle comes out clean.

MICROWAVE PEANUT BRITTLE

Cook on high heat 1 cup sugar, 1 cup raw peanuts, 1/2 cup Karo syrup, and 1/4 teaspoon salt. Cook 4 minutes. Take out and stir. Put back and cook about 3 minutes. Add 1 teaspoon margarine and 1 teaspoon vanilla. Put back and cook 1 1/2 minutes. Take out and add 1 teaspoon soda. Pour out on greased cookie sheet.

'NO TIME' COBBLER

Heat:

**2 1/2 cups canned peaches, pears,
or cherries with syrup**

Melt:

1/2 cup oleo in 8 x 8 dish in oven

Mix:

**1/2 cup flour
1/2 cup sugar
1 teaspoon baking powder
1/2 teaspoon salt
1/2 cup milk**

Pour flour mixture into melted butter when it begins to bubble. Pour the hot fruit over flour and butter mixture and cook about 30 minutes at 400 degrees until it browns.

COCONUT CUSTARD PIE

**2 1/4 cups sugar
1 1/4 cups milk
3 tablespoons flour
1 tablespoon vanilla extract
3 eggs
2 tablespoons butter
1 package coconut**

Combine eggs and sugar and beat well. Add all other ingredients, stirring until smooth. Pour into uncooked pie shell. Cook until toothpick inserted in the middle comes out clean.

FRIED FRUIT PIES

This recipe can be used with any dried fruit. Apples, peaches, apricots, prunes, etc.

Place 1 package of dried peaches into a deep saucepan. Cover with water and cook on medium heat until water cooks down and peaches are tender. Add sugar and set aside to cool.

Using a recipe for pie crust or dough, roll out pieces of dough approximately 3 x 5 inches and spoon peaches on dough, leaving 1 inch around the edges. Fold like a pocket. Use a fork to press the edges together. Fry in buttered skillet until golden brown on each side. Serve hot with ice cream or serve cold.

> *Taught to me by my mother, Mildred Lee. When we used apples or peaches, we would peel, slice, and lay them on pieces of tin out in the sun to dry. We would turn them frequently until all fruit was completely dry throughout. Then we would store until time for using.*

VINEGAR PIE

4 eggs
1 1/2 cups sugar
1/4 cup butter or margarine, melted
1 1/2 tablespoons cider or
   white vinegar
1 teaspoon vanilla

Preheat oven to 350 degrees. Combine all ingredients and mix well. Pour in 9-inch pie shell and bake until firm (about 50 minutes).

OLD FASHIONED SUGAR PIE

(The following recipe is said to be 150 years old.)

1 cup milk
1 cup brown sugar
3 tablespoons flour
1 egg
Pinch of salt

Beat well and pour into an 8-inch pie shell. Bake at 375 degrees for 25-30 minutes. Add 1 teaspoon butter flavoring, 1 teaspoon vanilla flavoring, and 1/4 cup shredded coconut (optional).

GOLDEN PECAN PIE

3/4 cup sugar
1 tablespoon all-purpose flour
Pinch of salt
3 eggs, well beaten
1 cup light corn syrup
1 teaspoon vanilla extract
2 tablespoons margarine, softened
1 cup pecan halves
1 unbaked 9-inch pastry shell

Combine dry ingredients in large mixing bowl. Add eggs, syrup, vanilla, and margarine. Beat well with electric mixer until blended. Stir in pecans. Pour mixture into pastry shell and bake at 350 degrees for 55 to 60 minutes. Yield: One 9-inch pie.

FRESH APPLE PIE

3 cups diced apples
2/3 cup sugar
1 tablespoon flour
1/4 teaspoon cinnamon
1/4 teaspoon nutmeg
2 tablespoons whole milk
2 tablespoons butter or margarine

Mix sugar, flour, and spices together and mix apples until well blended. Place mixture in unbaked pie crust. Add milk and dot butter or margarine over top. Place top pie crust over pie and fasten edges securely. Top with a little margarine or butter. Bake on cookie sheet in preheated oven at 400 degrees for 50 minutes. Yield: 8 servings.

FLAKY PIE CRUST

2 level cups all-purpose flour
3/4 cup Crisco
1 level teaspoon salt
5 tablespoons cold water

Cut Crisco into flour and salt until pea-sized chunks form. Sprinkle water a little a time. Toss with fork until dough will form a ball. Divide dough into two parts. Sprinkle flour on rolling pin and rolling surface. Roll into a circle and trim 1 inch larger than upside-down pie plate (I roll mine between 2 pieces of wax paper). Place one dough part in pie plate, add filling. Place top crust on, fold under bottom crust, and flute. Slit top crust to allow steam to escape.

Taught to me by my mother Mildred Lee.

CARAMEL PIE

2 cups sugar
1 teaspoon vanilla
1/4 cup butter
1/2 cup flour
2 cups sweet milk
4 eggs

Brown two-thirds cup sugar and butter in skillet, pour 1 cup (heated) milk in and cook slow. Mix other ingredients and pour into brown sugar. Cook until thick. Pour into unbaked crust and bake 30 minutes at 350 degrees.

Taught to me by my mother Mildred Lee.

FUDGE PIE

1 1/2 cups sugar
Pinch of salt
2 eggs
1 tablespoon vanilla
3 tablespoons cocoa
1 tablespoon flour
1/3 cup milk
1 stick of margarine,
    melted & cooled

Mix all dry ingredients – sugar, flour, cocoa, salt. Add slightly-beaten eggs, milk, and vanilla, mix well, then add margarine. Pour into unbaked pie shell. Bake 350 degrees for 45 minutes to one hour.

Taught to me by Jan Corrigan.

COCONUT PIE (1)

1 baked 9-inch pie shell
1 3/4 cups milk
2/3 cup sugar
1/4 teaspoon salt
1/4 cup flour
3 egg yolks, beaten
1 teaspoon vanilla
1/2 can Angel Flake coconut

Place milk in saucepan to scald. While it is scalding, sift together in saucepan the sugar, flour, and salt and gradually add to scalded milk. Place in a double boiler and cook, stirring constantly, for 8 to 10 minutes or until thick. Pour a little of this mixture over the egg yolks, stirring constantly, until all of liquid has been added. Now return to stove and cook for about 2 minutes longer. Set aside and, when cool, add vanilla and coconut. Pour into pie shell and top with meringue made from 3 egg whites. Sprinkle coconut over top of meringue and place in oven to brown.

MERINGUE

3 egg whites
Pinch of salt
6 tablespoons sugar
1/4 teaspoon vanilla

Beat egg whites until they are very stiff but not dry, then very gradually add the salt and sugar, beating all the while. Add the vanilla and continue to beat until the mixture is very creamy and smooth. Be sure when you top the pie that the meringue touches the crust of the pie all around.

COCONUT PIE (2)

4 eggs, separated
1/2 to 3/4 cup sugar
2 cups milk
1 teaspoon vanilla
1/2 stick butter
2 1/2 tablespoons cornstarch
Shredded coconut

Beat egg yolks, add sugar to yolks. Mix well. Mix cornstarch with 1/2 cup milk and add to mixture. Stir constantly over medium heat. Keep adding rest of milk a little at a time. Cook until thickens, and add 1/2 stick butter. Cook, stirring constantly until butter has melted and mixed well. Remove from heat and add vanilla and shredded coconut. Pour into baked pie shell. Beat egg whites and add small amount of sugar to taste. Spread over pie. Sprinkle coconut over top and brown in oven.

Taught to me by my mother-in-law Arah Richardson.

CHOCOLATE PIE (1)

1 cup sugar
1 egg
1 teaspoon vanilla flavoring
1 cup sweet milk
1/2 cup Hershey's cocoa
1 tablespoon flour
Dash of salt

Mix sugar, cocoa, and flour together. Add egg well beaten with milk. Cook over medium heat, stirring frequently. When thick add salt and flavoring. Makes 8-inch pie.

CHOCOLATE PIE (2)

1 1/4 cups sugar
3 egg yolks
2 cups milk
1/2 teaspoon vanilla
1 1/2 tablespoons cocoa
2 1/2 tablespoons flour

Mix dry ingredients. Add remaining ingredients. Cook in double boiler until thick as pudding. Pour in a baked pie shell and top with meringue.

Taught to me by Sandra & Gerald Jetton.

ICE BOX LEMON PIE
(my children's favorite)

2 cans of Eagle Brand milk
3/4 cup of water
5 fresh lemons, squeezed
1 package vanilla wafers

Mix in bowl, the 2 cans of milk, lemons, water. The mixture will thicken. Crumble 1 package of vanilla wafers in a pyrex dish. Pour mixture over the wafers and chill. Serve when cold.

CHESS PIE (1)

1 1/2 cups sugar
1 tablespoon cornmeal
1/2 cup melted margarine
3 whole eggs
1 tablespoon vinegar
1 teaspoon vanilla
1/2 cup milk
unbaked pie shell

Combine sugar with cornmeal, add margarine and cream well. Add eggs one at a time, cream thoroughly. Add vinegar, vanilla, then milk. Beat thoroughly. Bake in unbaked pie shell 10 minutes at 400 degrees, then reduce heat to 325 until done (approximately 45 minutes).

Taught to me by my mother Mildred Lee.

CHESS PIE (2)

1 tablespoon flour
2 cups sugar
3 eggs
1/2 stick oleo, melted
1/4 cup sweet milk
1 teaspoon vanilla
1 tablespoon cornmeal

Mix well. Pour in unbaked pie shell and bake 45 minutes at 300 degrees.

Taught to me by Sandra & Gerald Jetton.

RAISIN PIE

1 cup brown sugar
3 tablespoons cornstarch
3 tablespoons lemon juice
1 teaspoon grated lemon rind
2 cups raisins
1 1/3 cups water
1/16 teaspoon salt
1 tablespoon butter

Combine sugar, cornstarch, water, raisins, and lemon juice and cook until slightly thickened. Add lemon rind, salt, and butter. Pour into an 8 1/2-inch pastry-lined pie plate. Cover with latticed crust and flute edges. Bake in a preheated oven at 425 degrees for 40 minutes.

Taught to me by my mother Mildred Lee.

PEACHES AND CREAM PIE

1 9-inch unbaked pie shell
1 cup sugar
2 tablespoons cornstarch
4 cups peaches (fresh, peeled,
    and cut in quarters)
1 cup light or coffee cream

Fill pie shell with peaches. Mix sugar and cornstarch and sprinkle over peaches. Pour cream over all. Bake 1 hour at 375 degrees.

Taught to me by Bernice Jetton.

HOMEMADE ICE CREAM (1)

This very special ice cream recipe requires no cooking and was especially made to use with native Ozark fruits and nuts. Excellent with peaches, cherries, blueberries, etc., and becomes super-great when Ozark walnuts are added.

> **4 large eggs**
> **1 can condensed milk (recipe for**
> **homemade condensed milk below)**
> **1 1/2 cups sugar**
> **8 cups milk**
> **1 1/2 cups sweetened fruit**

Mix eggs, sugar, and four cups of milk until frothy. Add condensed milk and remaining milk, and mix some more. Add fruit and freeze. Makes one gallon in home freezer, electric or hand-crank.

To make your own condensed milk: Mix 3/4 cup dry milk and 1 cup sugar in 1/2 cup of warm water, stirring until graininess is almost gone. Let set until thick (about 6 hours) in refrigerator.

HOMEMADE ICE CREAM (2)

Combine in large bowl 2 cans of Eagle brand milk, 1 large can of Pet milk, 1/2 cup sugar, 1 teaspoon vanilla extract, and 2 cups homogenized milk. Depending on what flavor you want, 8 crushed bananas for banana ice cream, 2 cups crushed strawberries for strawberry ice cream, 2 cups diced fresh peaches for peach ice cream, or 2 cups blueberries for blueberry ice cream. Pour in freezer and freeze. After freezer stops and ice cream is finished, let set for 30 minutes before removing.

This is an old Itawamba County recipe. When I was growing up we made homemade ice cream on every special occasion and every chance we got. We would sit out under the shade trees and use a hand freezer. Sometimes we would put an old discarded cloth coated with used motor oil inside a used tin can and set fire to it to keep the bugs and insects away. The rag would not flame, just smolder, and the smoke kept all unwanted flying things from coming around and biting.

CHOCOLATE SAUCE

2 squares chocolate
1 cup water
2 cups sugar
Pinch salt
2 teaspoons vanilla
2 tablespoons butter
1/2 cup nuts, chopped

Cut the chocolate into pieces and add water. Place over the direct heat and stir constantly until thick and smooth. Add sugar and salt and stir until dissolved. Boil for 3 minutes, then add the vanilla and butter and add the nuts last.

Serve with ice cream.

Extras

MILK GRAVY

1/2 cup Crisco, melted
1/2 cup self-rising flour
2 cups sweet milk
Salt and pepper

Melt 1/2 cup Crisco into a large skillet. Pour in 1/2 cup of flour with salt and pepper. Cook on medium heat until flour is mixed well with Crisco and browned. Gradually mix in 2 cups of milk, turn on low heat, and stir until thick. Serve with breakfast or with potatoes, chicken, etc.

My husband makes this and if he doesn't want it plain he will add sausage to it or sometimes chopped-up Vienna sausage. This way you don't have to cook a breakfast meat. It's super!

RED EYE GRAVY

This gravy can only be made by first frying 6-8 pieces of Country Ham in approximately 1/4 cup cooking oil. Remove the ham from the frying pan and reduce heat to low. Pour 1 cup electric perked coffee into skillet. Let simmer about 5 minutes.

This is great served with grits and hot biscuits for breakfast. Red eye gravy is often called sawmill gravy. When I was young and my mother and I lived with her parents, my grandfather made this every morning. He ran a sawmill and had several men working for him. They would come into our home very early every morning and sit around the fireplace dipping snuff. Carolyn and I had to dress for school in a cold room without heat.

CORNBREAD DRESSING

4 eggs, boiled and chopped
4 cups of crumbled cornbread
4 cups of chicken stock
1 cup melted butter
3/4 cup diced onion
1/2 cup diced celery
1/4 cup of sage

Mix all ingredients together and pour into greased ovenproof dish. Bake at 375-400 degrees for approximately 45 minutes or until brown.

I've eaten many kinds of dressings and stuffings but there's no dressing like cornbread dressing. On a holiday once we were having Thanksgiving dinner with some friends. She began to prepare the dressing and it dawned on me that I didn't like her dressing. I told her I would help with the dinner but would she please let my mother cook the dressing. It was great!

SHRIMP-RICE CASSEROLE

1 1/2 cups instant rice
1 teaspoon curry powder
1 teaspoon salt
1 1/2 cups water
2 lbs. cooked shrimp
1 green pepper
4 slices pineapple
1 can cream of celery soup

Cook rice until done with salt in water. Stir in curry powder. Mix green pepper, diced pineapple, and shrimp together. Then add celery soup and bake in 350-degree oven for 30 minutes. Serves 8.

This is a dish I learned to cook while traveling in the state of Louisiana. It's great to serve outside on the patio in the summer. My children love rice instead of potatoes for a change.

CHILI-CON-CARNE

2 cans tomatoes, blended
1/2 teaspoon salt
3 cans red kidney beans
1 medium onion, chopped
1 bell pepper, chopped
2 cans tomato sauce
1 lb. lean ground pork
1 lb. lean ground beef
Chili powder
1/2 teaspoon pepper

Sauté onion, pepper, beef, and pork. Drain off juices. Add tomatoes, tomato sauce, and beans. Mix well. Add salt, pepper, and chili powder to taste. Cook on low with lid on pot. Add chili powder a little at a time and taste until you get the desired amount you like.

Taught to me by my mother Mildred Lee.

PIMENTO CHEESE SPREAD

1/3 cup sweet milk
2 4 oz. cans pimento
3 tablespoons sugar
1 egg, beaten
2 tablespoons vinegar
1 lb. American cheese, grated

Mix milk, pimento, sugar, and egg into double boiler and cook until cheese melts. Add vinegar. Cool. Add pint of your favorite salad dressing. Store in refrigerator.

> *My daughter Jackie could live on this spread. It's so much better than what you buy in the stores. This is one of the first recipes she asked for when she got married eight years ago.*

PIMENTO SANDWICH FILLING

Chop fine:

1/2 lb. mild cheese
2 hard-boiled eggs
1 cup pimentos

Combine:

1/2 cup milk
3 tablespoons vinegar
1 egg, beaten
1 tablespoon flour

Cook in double boiler until thickened, then add to chopped ingredients while hot. Mix. Can be used for sandwiches warm or after stored in refrigerator.

HAZEL'S HOT DOG MIX

1 16 oz. package shredded kraut
1/2 cup ketchup
1 teaspoon paprika
1 medium bell pepper, chopped
1/2 cup chili sauce
Juice of 1 lemon
1 medium chopped onion
1/4 cup sugar

Drain juice off kraut, then mix with other ingredients. Cover and refrigerate for 1 hour before using. This mix makes delicious dressing for hot dogs. Will keep for over a week.

The little town of Red Bay, Alabama was my second home and Hazel Hall (my cousin) was my second mama. I spent half my time at her house with her daughter Jane, son Jimmy, and husband Dan. She is still today one of my very favorite cooks (and Dan too). After mother, she comes next.

SAUSAGE BALLS

3 cups Bisquick
2 cups grated cheese
1 lb. hot sausage

Mix ingredients together and form into balls. Bake at 400 degrees for about 15 or 20 minutes.

Taught to me by my mother Mildred Lee.

BARBECUE SAUCE

1 cup water
1/2 cup vinegar
4 tablespoons sugar
1 tablespoon prepared mustard
3/4 teaspoon black pepper
1/2 teaspoon red pepper
1 tablespoon salt
1 large onion, chopped
1 lemon, cut in half
1 stick butter or oleo

Mix ingredients and simmer for 20 minutes. Remove lemon rind and add:

1 cup tomato catsup
5 teaspoons Worcestershire sauce

Bring to boil and use. Will keep in refrigerator for weeks.

Taught to me by my mother Mildred Lee.

TUNA DIP

1 6 oz. can of white tuna, drained
2 eggs, hard-boiled
1 package Italian salad dressing mix
1 cup sour cream
3 tablespoons bacon bits

Mix dressing and sour cream, then add diced egg, tuna, and bacon bits. Stir until blended and chill. Serve with chips or crackers.

CLAM DIP

1 can chopped clams
8 oz. sour cream
1 clove garlic
1/2 onion, chopped fine
1/4 teaspoon lemon juice

Drain juice from the clams. Press garlic. Add clams, sour cream, garlic, onion, and lemon juice. Mix well. It's better if you let it sit for a few hours. The sour cream will mold better if it's not fresh.

Taught to me by my friend Cleta Hillygus.

FRESH PINEAPPLE DIP

1 fresh pineapple (choose one
**   with nice top)**
1 teaspoon all-purpose flour
Assorted fruit for dipping
1 egg, well beaten
3 to 4 tablespoons sugar
8 oz. whipping cream or Cool Whip

Cut pineapple in half lengthwise, removing the nice chunks for dipping. Scoop out the pulp leaving shell 1/2 inch thick. Set shell aside. Chop pineapple into bite size pieces, discarding core. Reserve half of the pineapple pieces for dipping and crush the others. Combine sugar, flour, beaten egg, crushed pineapple, and juice in saucepan. Cook over low heat until thickened. Cool. Fold in whipped cream and spoon into pineapple shell. Serve dip with pineapple chunks and other fresh fruit. For additional pineapple chunks use "Lite" canned pineapple in own juice.

Taught to me by my friend Cleta Hillygus.

CREAM CHEESE DIPS

**1 8-oz. package Philadelphia
  cream cheese
1 teaspoon onion juice
1 tablespoon mayonnaise
1/4 cup milk
1 tablespoon Worcestershire sauce**

Mix cream cheese and onion juice. Add other ingredients to proper consistency.

CURRY DIP

**1/2 cup mayonnaise
1 cup sour cream
2 tablespoons lemon juice
1 teaspoon curry powder
1/2 teaspoon paprika
1/2 cup diced onion
2 teaspoons hot mustard
2 dashes Tabasco sauce
2 dashes Worcestershire sauce
salt and pepper**

Mix well, blend and chill overnight.

AVOCADO DIP

4 avocados
1 large tomato
1/4 jar salsa (hot)
Salt to taste
1 large onion
1 small can chopped green chilés
1 clove garlic

Mash avocados, chop onions and tomato fine, press garlic, and drain chopped green chilés. Mix all ingredients. Serve with tortilla chips.

Taught to me by my friend Cleta Hillygus.

SOUR CREAM DRESSING

1 pint package sour cream
1/2 cup white wine vinegar
1/3 cup of red wine vinegar

Mix ingredients and let stand overnight. Use on any green salad.

FRENCH DRESSING (1)

1 cup tomato soup
1 cup vinegar
1 cup oil
1 package old fashioned seasoning
1 tablespoon grated cheese
1 cup sugar
Grated onion or garlic

Mix thoroughly for salads.

Taught to me by Mrs. Rosell Brewer.

FRENCH DRESSING (2)

2 cups salad oil
1 cup vinegar
1 cup catsup
1 grated onion
4 tablespoons sugar
1 teaspoon salt
1 teaspoon paprika
1 garlic bud, chopped fine

Blend in blender or with mixer.

Variation: Add a wedge of Roquefort cheese before blending.

FRENCH DRESSING (3)

1/2 cup oil
2 tablespoons vinegar
2 tablespoons lemon juice
3/4 teaspoon salt
1/2 teaspoon paprika
1/2 teaspoon mustard
1 teaspoon powdered sugar
Dash of cayenne pepper

Combine all ingredients and store in refrigerator indefinitely.

THOUSAND ISLAND DRESSING

1 medium-sized sweet onion,
  chopped
1 medium-sized mango, chopped
1/2 cup pickle relish
1/4 cup olives, chopped
6 hard-boiled eggs, chopped
1 quart mayonnaise
12 oz. size chili sauce

Combine all ingredients and store in refrigerator indefinitely.

THAT'S FREEZE PEACH JAM

Flavor of fresh peaches! Peach Jam is plain and simple. Spicy Peach Jam is enhanced with orange juice and rind as well as cloves. Both recipes are easy to prepare and make several containers of jam.

**1 1/2 cups prepared fruit (about
1 1/4 lb. fully ripe peaches)
3 tablespoons lemon juice
1/2 teaspoon ascorbic acid crystals
(optional)
3 1/4 cups (1 lb. 6 oz.) sugar
1 pouch Certo fruit pectin**

First prepare the fruit. Peel and pit about 1 1/4 pounds peaches. Chop very fine or grind. Measure 1 1/2 cups into large bowl or pan. Add ascorbic acid crystals.

Then make the jam. Thoroughly mix sugar into fruit. Let stand 10 minutes. Add lemon juice to fruit pectin in small bowl. Stir into fruit. Continue stirring 3 minutes. (A few sugar crystals will remain.) Ladle quickly into scalded containers, filling to within 1/2 inch of tops. Cover at once with tight lids. Let stand at room temperature 24 hours, then store in freezer. Small amounts may be covered and stored in refrigerator up to 3 weeks. Makes about 3 2/3 cups or about 5 (8 fl. oz.) containers.

Taught to me by my sister-in-law Marie Meier.

Index